ASHE Higher Education Report: Volume 34, Number 2
Kelly Ward, Lisa E. Wolf-Wendel, Series Editors

D0791794

Selling Higher Education: Marketing and Advertising America's Colleges and Universities

Eric J. Anctil

Selling Higher Education: Marketing and Advertising America's
Colleges and Universities
Eric J. Anctil
ASHE Higher Education Report: Volume 34, Number 2
Kelly Ward, Lisa E. Wolf-Wendel, Series Editors

ISSN 1551-6970   electronic ISSN 1554-6306   ISBN 978-0-4704-3773-5

The ASHE Higher Education Report is part of the Jossey-Bass Higher and Adult
Education Series and is published six times a year by Wiley Subscription Services,
Inc., A Wiley Company, at Jossey-Bass, 989 Market Street, San Francisco,
California 94103-1741.

For subscription information, see the Back Issue/Subscription Order Form
in the back of this volume.

CALL FOR PROPOSALS: Prospective authors are strongly encouraged to contact
Kelly Ward (kaward@wsu.edu) or Lisa Wolf-Wendel (lwolf@ku.edu). See "About
the ASHE Higher Education Report Series" in the back of this volume.

Visit the Jossey-Bass Web site at **www.josseybass.com.**

The ASHE Higher Education Report is indexed in CIJE: Current Index to Jour-
nals in Education (ERIC), Current Abstracts (EBSCO), Education Index/Abstracts
(H.W. Wilson), ERIC Database (Education Resources Information Center),
Higher Education Abstracts (Claremont Graduate University), IBR & IBZ: Inter-
national Bibliographies of Periodical Literature (K.G. Saur), and Resources in
Education (ERIC).

Advisory Board

Contents

Executive Summary

Until the latter part of the twentieth century, the mission of higher education could largely remain fixed on advancing the public trust in our colleges and universities, regardless of size, type, or mission, by delivering sound academic programs, conducting and promoting research, and engaging with the community. The world of higher education has changed too dramatically, however, for institutions not to reframe themselves as both education *and* business institutions. Generally, it has already occurred, and many colleges and universities have redefined how they do the "business" of providing higher education. The past fifteen years has seen marketing departments emerge on campuses to represent the entire institution and, on some larger campuses, individual units (specific colleges, a foundation, or alumni relations).

Now that most colleges and universities operate a business model that employs marketing and advertising principles and practices, decisions must be made that illustrate the differences between marketing for business and marketing for education. Like business, education can be responsive to the market, but its sense of self extends beyond satisfying market needs. Education is mission driven precisely because its mission is *not* business; its mission is providing higher education as a social institution.

State appropriations for higher education have steadily decreased in the past forty years as competition from for-profit education providers such as the University of Phoenix has increased. Something has had to replace this loss of income and meet the demands of a more competitive higher education marketplace. Market income has increasingly substituted for public appropriations in higher education, which has fundamentally changed the core identity and mission of many colleges and universities, especially public institutions. For the modern university to remain viable and essential to advancing the public trust, it must be attentive to how the market positively affects it. In this paradigm, the market *supports* and *propels* the mission rather than obstructs it.

Successful marketing of colleges and universities aims to be both mission driven and market driven. The institution and those charged with running it must have faith in what they do and who they are. But they also must be attentive to the market and employ sound marketing practices to determine current market demands and how to address, deliver, and satisfy them.

The main purpose of this monograph is to present the relevant research and literature on marketing and advertising higher education and, at the same time, interweave general marketing and advertising theory and practice in an attempt to explain why the business side of higher education behaves as it does and to recommend solutions to administrators, policymakers, and other key stakeholders. Marketing and advertising theory, research, and general scholarship are enormous fields from which important theories and practices have been drawn and applied to the business of marketing and advertising of higher education. These ideas have been selected to give a broad perspective on marketing as well as to offer specific suggestions and direction about how best to apply this information to specific contexts.

The second body of literature in this monograph addresses how colleges and universities market their intangible qualities. Much of what is "for sale" in higher education are intangibles such as learning and lived experiences. It is impossible to truly show a prospective student what a college education is, so colleges and universities often show the evidence of what a college education experience will look like.

Coupled with the marketing and advertising literature is a presentation of college choice theory and a discussion of the Elaboration Likelihood Model (Petty and Cacioppo, 1981, 1984a, 1984b, 1986a, 1986b), which is used to explain how consumers are often persuaded to make purchasing choices that provide a context for college and university marketing units' behavior when attempting to persuade students to enroll in an institution or others to support the organization more broadly.

Today's colleges and universities must strike a balance between advancing the public trust as social institutions and places of higher learning while also being mindful of the contemporary challenges of running large organizations with dwindling public support and greater competition from the for-profit education sector. Colleges and universities that are not only aware of this environment but also are savvy in the changing marketplace increase their chances of establishing distinction among their peers. Strong institutional identity requires clearly recognizing one's organizational strengths, effectively communicating how one is different in a crowded marketplace, and building collaborative partnerships internally and externally to promote greater awareness and recognition among key stakeholders. Strategic marketing enables one to move from being simply *driven* by the market to being *savvy* about it. Confronting an era marked by dwindling support and increased competition, administrators and higher education leaders at colleges and universities must broadcast who they are, what they do, and what makes them valuable. The business of higher education depends on it.

Foreword

I recently viewed a satiric online advertisement for a made-up university, Quendleton State University (QSU). The ad looks like a "typical" television spot for a college, one you might see while watching an NCAA sporting event. This ad, however, was not real. The video enumerates the wonders of QSU, showing students studying together, working with professors, and enjoying the campus community. The campus seems idyllic—the kind of place anyone would want to attend, work, or make donations to. The voice-overs, however, tell a different story. We learn, for example, that *U.S. News and World Report* rates the school as "adequate" and that the diversity represented in the pictures is merely for show. The closing line for the ad is perfect: "if we were a good university we wouldn't have a commercial." The QSU video is funny and appealing because we as academics are conditioned to expect to see catchy jingles, slogans, and idyllic images of campuses rather than talk about the realities of higher education. The marketing of higher education has risen to the level of satire: what a confirmation that higher education marketing has arrived!

Perhaps I am naive, but a part of me wants to believe that institutions of higher education should not need to worry about image, let alone attempt to market themselves. Those that do must be lower-quality institutions. Still, reading the present monograph by Eric Anctil helped me to see the inevitability of marketing in higher education along with its more positive attributes. The monograph uses literature from higher education, marketing, advertising, and business to show why and how institutions of higher education are marketing themselves. From this monograph I learned that some investment in these activities can further the educational goals of academic institutions and can help institutions control their own destinies. I learned about the various audiences that institutions of higher education need to reach—students, policymakers, donors, alumni, sports fans, and employees—and how to tailor one's marketing to each particular niche. I also learned that everyone is doing it: public and private institutions, the elite and the less than elite. And I learned some of the more effective practices institutions can use to "sell" themselves without selling out.

In light of this monograph, I thought about my own institution's recent foray into the world of higher education branding and marketing. The University of Kansas hired expensive consultants to figure out how to better communicate our message to our constituents. The consultants told us, among other things, that we needed a more coherent visual identity and a new font for our initials; we learned too late that Kutztown State University already was using the same initials with the same font: a hard lesson that there are consequences for not knowing one's position in the market! We were also told that we needed new advertisements with catchy jingles showing the diversity of our school, highlighting our athletic success, and showing students graduating. Our Web sites and our business cards and letterhead, said the consultants, did not look enough alike. The consultants even suggested that the Jayhawk (our mascot) was not an academic enough symbol and that we ought to use it less (we did not listen to them on that one). Still, the institution has endeavored to market itself more effectively. Some of these changes make sense to me; some seem less essential. The cynic in me still asks, "If we were a really good school, would we need to do these things?" The realist in me knows the answer is "yes." The good news is that, done right, advertising and marketing of higher education can help us better deliver high-quality education and can actually make an institution better.

This monograph guides us in learning how to think more positively about marketing and advertising and how to do it more effectively. The monograph is written for numerous audiences: administrators who need to consider how the institution is being perceived, marketing and public relations officers who need to improve the institution's message, and cynical faculty who wish we did not have to worry about such nonacademic matters. The lessons are in here and they are important to heed. A person can celebrate an institution's academic mission while cheering on the mascot. We can advance scholarship and market it too. Rock Chalk Jayhawk. Go KU!

Lisa E. Wolf-Wendel
Series Editor

Acknowledgments

I would like to thank Kelly Ward and Lisa Wolf-Wendel for their tireless patience and constructive feedback from the initial proposal of this monograph to its completion. Kelly is a dear friend and a wonderful colleague, and I owe her more than can be captured on this page for her friendship and also for her support as a mentor. And thank you, Lisa, for reading this monograph more times than any one person should have to.

This monograph benefited greatly from collaborative input from Bradford Zulick and Narayan Devanathan. They both offered invaluable information and feedback in the initial stages of development, and the monograph would not be what it is today without them.

Thank you also to the several colleagues who served as referees for this monograph. Your feedback—positive and constructive, substantive and technical—influenced the quality of the finished product, and I am grateful for your considerable time and the thoughtfulness of your critiques.

Finally, thank you to my wife, Tina, and my boys, Jack and Benjamin— my three favorite people with whom to experience life and a baseball game.

Published online in Wiley InterScience
(www.interscience.wiley.com) • DOI: 10.1002/aehe.3402

Market Driven Versus Mission Driven

S HOULD COLLEGES AND UNIVERSITIES be driven by mission or the market? Sands and Smith (1999) believe this question sits at the heart of the long-standing debate in higher education marketing. "Most often stated as an either-or proposition, this debate immediately pits the faculty and its leadership, who have responsibility for the curriculum and academic program of an institution, against the administrative staff charged with marketing it" (p. 43). A comprehensive examination of the literature in the area of higher education marketing and advertising literature confirms that much of the conversation about marketing (and, similarly, advertising) higher education is about trying to determine what higher education is, what function it serves, and how best to communicate this information to various interest groups and stakeholders.

Opinions abound in the conversation about what exactly "marketing of higher education" is and what it should be. On the one hand are the supposed proponents of marketing and advertising higher education: the administrative staff responsible for recruiting and retaining students, soliciting donations and in-kind support, and projecting an institutional image that contributes to those endeavors. On the other hand are the supposed academics and students who are purportedly uncomfortable talking about higher education as big business and do not believe the two can (or should) harmoniously exist. (It is not uncommon in the nonacademic literature to read quotes from professors decrying the modern university's slow descent into commercialism and the loss of academic values in the process. Although the assumption seems to be that liberal arts professors are at the forefront of this resistance to the changing university, the evidence for this characterization is weak at best and seems to be perpetuated by those writing on the topic rather than as an observable phenomenon.)

Both these depictions seem to be gross caricatures of the current higher education landscape. The challenge for higher education does not lie in bringing these two disparate sides into agreement; the challenge lies in positioning colleges and universities as social institutions, with missions dedicated to the public good, while at the same time remaining viable institutions both financially and in the open marketplace. Although many academics and others may wish colleges and universities could operate chiefly as the educational institutions they have been imagined to be, the reality is that higher education is now big business: the way to remain viable and thrive in the open marketplace is to accept the already shifted paradigm and learn to work in the new higher education environment. Similarly, campus administrators have to recognize the important contributions faculty, staff, and students make toward creating a campus culture that defines and promotes a strong institutional message that can be used to guide the organization as well as an element of effect marketing strategy (Toma, Dubrow, and Hartley, 2005).

As we will see, the higher education landscape has changed significantly over the past forty years, and colleges and universities have had to be adaptive and responsive to entirely new expectations and changing financial realities. Public funding for state schools has declined significantly from the 1950s and 1960s, student populations have ebbed and flowed with each generation and competition for students has increased right along with them, and recently higher education has been called on to be more accountable for its work educating college students (Dillon, 2006).

Given this context, debate continues about what exactly higher education is. At various times it is the product, a service provider, or a product vendor and a service provider. Likewise, students are characterized as consumers *and* products intermittently and together, which introduces a strange kind of economics when one considers how important it is to recruit and retain students who will then be part of the quality measurements used to evaluate the value of the product itself (Edmondson, 1987; Winston, 1999).

Colleges and universities could be said to be selling a product (a degree) and the services they provide (teaching and learning, social life, goods) are simply accessories designed to enhance the perceived (and real) value of the product. One could argue that the better the quality of service enhancements, the better the quality of the product itself. After all, a degree is really just paper documenting an experience—an experience colleges and universities hope will have a lasting impact on the student who experienced it and will lead to a lifetime of interactions that will translate to alumni donations, state support, and positive opinions to others interested in purchasing the same experience.

Edmondson writes that college is "a peculiar industry where the customer is also the product—and what the customer wants may not always be the best for the product" (1987, p. 27). Students, then, are the product of education *and* they are its customers. And because they are customers, they are targeted by advertising the same way potential buyers of sneakers or cars are targeted. They are susceptible to persuasion. They are fickle consumers who demand a good price, a good value, and a quality product or experience. And, finally, they form relationships to colleges and universities in brand communities (McAlexander, Koenig, and Schouten, 2004), not unlike those formed around iPods or Mini Coopers.

Market Driven *and* Mission Driven

Until the latter part of the twentieth century, the mission of higher education could largely remain fixed on advancing the public trust with our colleges and universities by delivering sound academic programs, conducting and promoting research, and engaging with the community, regardless of size, type, or mission. The world of higher education has changed too dramatically, however, for institutions not to reframe themselves as both education *and* business institutions. Generally, this change has already occurred, and many colleges and universities have redefined how they do the "business" of providing higher education. The past fifteen years have seen marketing departments emerge on campuses to represent the entire institution and, on some larger campuses, individual units (for example, the business college, the college of education, and the nursing school each have their own marketing department) (Blumenstyk, 2006).

Now that most colleges and universities operate using a business model that employs marketing and advertising principles and practices, certain decisions have to be made that illustrate the differences between marketing for business and marketing for education. This dilemma brings us back to the question that opened this section: Should colleges and universities be driven by mission or by the market? This question is easy for businesses hoping to sell as many products or services as possible. They have to allow for their mission to be largely shaped by the market. If the mission that created widgets does not sell widgets, the mission or the widgets must be changed wholesale to satisfy market demands. But education is different. Education is not selling widgets that can be easily changed to meet the market's needs. Education can be responsive, but its sense of self extends beyond satisfying market needs. Education is mission driven precisely because its mission is *not* business; it provides higher education as a social institution.

The answer to whether higher education should be mission driven or market driven lies somewhere in the middle and is shaped by the economics of higher education in the modern era. State appropriations for higher education have steadily decreased in the past forty years (Bok, 2003; Zemsky, Wegner, and Massy, 2005). Something has had to replace this loss; market income has increasingly substituted for public appropriations in higher education, which has fundamentally changed the core identity and mission of many colleges and universities, especially public institutions. Zemsky, Wegner, and Massy (2005) assert that "the key to making the modern university more publicly relevant ironically lies in making it more market sensitive—or, to use the term we have come to favor, making the university more market-smart" (p. 7). This application of market income to fund programs essential to an institution's identity is what they believe is critical to remain "places of public pursuit" (p. 9). Zemsky, Wegner, and Massy label it "being market-smart to remain mission-centered" (p. 9). Rather than seeing the argument as an "either-or," they insist that for the modern university to remain viable and essential to advancing the public trust, it must be attentive to how the market positively affects it as well as sensitive to its core mission and values. In this paradigm, the market *supports* and *propels* the mission, rather than obstructing it.

Successful marketing of colleges and universities does not require answering an either-or question; rather, successful marketing of higher education aims to be both mission driven *and* market driven. The institution, and those charged with running it, must have faith in what they do and who they are.

But they also have to be attentive to the market and employ sound marketing practices to determine current market demands and how to address, deliver, and satisfy them.

Rather than engaging in a product-versus-service argument, Canterbury (1999) recommends a concept of higher education that is "product as opportunity," which he believes puts the responsibility on the student to take advantage of the opportunities afforded by a college or university while at the same time allows colleges and universities to market and advertise the opportunities that await a student at their institution rather than the "puffery" that he claims is common in so much marketing literature. I agree and hope you will read this monograph in that spirit. I believe colleges and universities do offer product as opportunity, which advances the public good *and* serves their collective mission. I also believe that in an era marked by dwindling support for all education, and higher education in particular, it is incumbent on administrators and higher education leaders at colleges and universities to broadcast who they are, what they do, and what makes them valuable. The business of higher education depends on it, as does the community.

Purpose and Structure of the Monograph

This monograph's main purpose is to present the relevant research and literature on marketing and advertising higher education; at the same time, it interweaves general marketing and advertising theory and practice in an attempt to explain why the business side of higher education behaves as it does, and it makes recommendations to administrators, policymakers, and other key stakeholders in higher education.

Marketing and advertising theory, research, and general scholarship are enormous fields unto themselves; to cover even a small portion of them thoroughly would be a daunting task. I have taken, however, what I believe are important theories and practices from that literature that can be applied to the business of marketing and advertising higher education. These ideas have been selected to give a broad perspective on marketing as well as to offer specific suggestions and direction about how best to apply this information to specific contexts.

The second body of literature in this monograph addresses how colleges and universities market their intangible qualities. Much of what is "for sale" in higher education are the intangibles such as learning and lived experiences. It is impossible to show a prospective student what a college education is, so colleges and universities often show the evidence of what a college education experience will look like.

Coupled with the marketing and advertising literature is a presentation of college choice theory and a discussion of the Elaboration Likelihood Model (Petty and Cacioppo, 1981, 1984a, 1984b, 1986a, 1986b), which is used to explain how consumers are often persuaded to make purchasing choices and provides a context for college and university marketing units' behavior when attempting to persuade students to enroll in an institution or others to support the organization more broadly.

This complicated conversation is made all the more complex given the size and scope of postsecondary education. Postsecondary education includes vocational schools, community and technical colleges, liberal arts colleges (mostly private), regional and state colleges, and research universities (both public and private), all with different purposes and missions, and serving different populations and communities. In addition to these traditional institutions are the emerging and well-established online higher education providers and other for-profit institutions. Whether they belong in the same category as the others just listed is an argument for another day, but one must appreciate their influence on the marketing and advertising of higher education.

Coupled with this diverse landscape of institutional type, size, and purpose are differences in each institutional type. Some liberal arts colleges boast strong sports programs, while others give little attention to such things. Some community colleges serve tens of thousands of students drawn from a large metropolitan area, while others serve a very narrow population sprinkled across a rural landscape. The institutional needs of these schools, based on their location and student population, are vastly different. This situation becomes even more complicated when the conversation includes research universities, regional colleges, and elite privates; the complexity of issues on institutional type alone is dizzying. Because of those inherent differences, writing about marketing and advertising for *all* of postsecondary education becomes very challenging if the goal is to address the individual needs of each institutional type or even just to address the categorical differences that exist among the same type of institutions.

To satisfy the range of possibilities, some common language is used throughout the monograph. The use of the terms "institutions of higher education" or "higher education" or "colleges and universities" reflects an almost universal adherence to those designations in the literature. Unless a writer is referring to a specific institutional type for a specific reason, he or she often groups all postsecondary institutions together and calls them "colleges" or "universities" or writes things like "higher education responded to the pressure. . . ."

Most of what is written here can be generally applied to the various institutional types we commonly think of when discussing postsecondary education (the discussion regarding the difference between the concept of "postsecondary education" and "higher education" will have to be saved for another day). Unless a specific institutional type is mentioned directly, the reader may assume that "colleges" and "universities" and "institutions of higher education" are catchall phrases for most institutional types.

Significance to Higher Education Study and Practice

This monograph is intended to serve a wide audience of readers—faculty, researchers, graduate students, campus administrators, department chairs, deans, provosts, presidents, directors of faculty development, directors of extension, and directors for centers for community and campus partnerships. In addition, extended audiences include communications and marketing personnel at colleges and universities and the advertising consultants they often use.

For the past forty years, colleges and universities have had to redefine who they are and whom they serve, and remain solvent despite financial challenges. The changing orientation of higher education into businesses creates demand on campus personnel to be fluent in the language and practice, which then makes for good business practice. This monograph addresses current advertising and marketing practices and the implications for higher education stakeholders to best prepare campus administrators and faculty in confronting the evermore competitive world of higher education in the twenty-first century. As the topic of marketing and advertising higher education attracts the attention of contemporary faculty and administrators, it should be of interest to those involved in creating and evaluating marketing and advertising practices on campuses around the country as a means not only to survive but also to prosper.

Persuasion and Choice

THIS CHAPTER PRESENTS TWO CRITICAL ELEMENTS in the selling of higher education: persuading someone that something you have is worth purchasing, and the process purchasers go through as they seek to buy it, from you or from one of your competitors. How one goes about choosing a college to attend is a complicated process that depends on multiple informational inputs (opinions from peers and parents, available information from different schools) as well as constraining factors (one's ability to pay for college, campus location). The chapter opens with a review of the literature on college choice and then moves into a discussion of how colleges and universities are part of a "trust economy" (Winston, 1999) in which buyers must trust that what they purchase will be delivered (a quality education, for example). A trust economy demands that colleges and universities effectively communicate who they are and what they do for those who invest in them. The chapter closes with a discussion of the Elaboration Likelihood Model of persuasion advanced by Petty and Cacioppo (1981). In this model, "elaboration" refers to the extent the receiver modifies his or her thoughts about a given message (in essence, does a person give the message more thought?), and "likelihood" refers to the probability that elaboration is likely or unlikely. The model attempts to explain situations that are likely to make people elaborate or not elaborate on a particular issue or message. As seen through the lens of the Elaboration Likelihood Model, marketing and advertising by colleges and universities should be targeted to both engage prospective students while they are in the process of choosing a college and create opportunities for prospective students to elaborate on the institutional message offered.

College Choice

The literature on college choice covers a wide range of topics and employs a variety of methodologies, all seeking to measure the factors that contribute to initial thought about college attendance and actual enrollment (Hossler, Braxton, and Coopersmith, 1989). In this broad area of research, two themes emerge that best illuminate the choice process and its relationship to how colleges and universities market and advertise themselves: (1) college choice is a long, developmental process with a variety of informational inputs that shape college and university choice sets, perceptions about particular institutions, and prospective student actions; and (2) research indicates how many constraining variables exist for many prospective applicants and how their decisions are largely shaped by forces that extend beyond interest or motivation. For example, according to a recent survey, 56 percent of students attend a school located within one hundred miles of home (Chute, 2006) and are limited by socioeconomic realities such as financial aid, which further limits their choices (Cabrera and La Nasa, 2000).

Nevertheless, the choice literature can tell us much about who (or what) influences a prospective applicant when it comes to thinking about college attendance, what motivates the student to seek out information about a particular school, and what ultimately leads to the student's enrollment.

Chapman's model of student college choice (1981) provides a comprehensive road map of the choice process. In his model, college choice is often predicated on the influence of significant persons such as parents, friends, high school personnel, and role models. These significant actors all contribute to how a student perceives various colleges and universities. In addition, Chapman's model indicates that the efforts made by a college or university have a direct effect on shaping student perspectives. Likewise, the fixed characteristics of the institution play a significant role in the selection process. These fixed characteristics include cost, location, the availability of financial aid, and the variety and availability of particular academic programs. Chapman's model indicates that it is the combination of fixed characteristics combined with the influence of significant people and the efforts made by colleges and universities to communicate with prospective students that ultimately leads to schools placed into the choice set and the eventual final choice for the enrollee.

The literature in the area of college choice suggests that the college choice process for high school seniors is actually a three-step process that begins as early as the seventh grade (Cabrera and La Nasa, 2000; Hossler, Braxton, and Coopersmith, 1989). "In undergoing each phase of the college-choice process, high school students develop predispositions to attend college, search for general information about college, and make choices leading them to enroll at a given institution of higher education" (Cabrera and La Nasa, 2000, p. 5). The three steps of the process (Cabrera and La Nasa, 2000; Chapman, 1981; Hossler and Gallagher, 1987; Jackson, 1982; Litten, 1982) can be thought of as follows:

The Predispositional Stage: The developmental stage that occurs in roughly grades seven to nine and includes parental encouragement and involvement, parental collegiate experience, and socioeconomic status.

The Search Stage: Accumulating and assessing the attributes of various postsecondary institutions. Includes considerations for socioeconomic status, occupational aspirations, educational aspirations. Identification of colleges and universities that can stand apart from others in this stage is critical. Generally occurs in grades ten to twelve.

The Choice Stage: Generating and narrowing the choice set, making the final decision based on perceived institutional attributes and perceived ability to cover cost. Occurs in grades eleven and twelve.

Many factors contribute to a student's final choice of a college or university (or whether to enroll at all). Beginning early in the college planning process, parental encouragement and involvement are critical (Cabrera and La Nasa, 2000; Conklin and Dailey, 1981; Hossler, Schmit, and Vesper, 1999; Stage and Hossler, 1989). Parents serve two functions: (1) to encourage thinking about eventual college choice by introducing the idea of higher education attendance and the preliminary choice set of possible schools; and (2) to assume an active role in preparing for that action by discussing college plans, taking steps to ensure their child is academically prepared, and saving for college (Henderson and Berla, 1994; Hossler and Vesper, 1993; Hossler, Schmit, and Vesper, 1999; Stage and Hossler, 1989). It is obvious that parents are critically important at every step of the choice process, which explains why so much of the marketing for recruitment is aimed at them. Not only do they often help fund the education; they also shape the very choices to be made and encourage the student through the process.

In addition to parental involvement, other factors play an important role as students go through the choice process. College size, location, academic offerings, reputation, prestige, selectivity, and significant alumni are all variables that are measured and evaluated. Finally, a student's peers, friends, and high school personnel—specifically the school counselor—influence the selection process, with financial considerations often guiding the final choice (Cabrera and La Nasa, 2000; Hossler, Braxton, and Coopersmith, 1989; Manski and Wise, 1983; Zemksy and Oedel, 1983).

Beyond College Choice: Building Trust and Engaging Stakeholders

Given the diversity of factors that influence college choice for the college bound, it is critical that colleges and universities understand the relationships they have with various key stakeholders and communicate with them core values of the institution's identity. Stakeholders can be engaged through advertising, and their engagement is often predicated on building trust for a product that is "purchased" but remains largely intangible.

As nonprofits, colleges and universities must behave as other nonprofits do when gathering support for their efforts. Building off the work of Hansmann (1980), Winston (1999) discusses the nonprofit sector's obligation to buyers who rely much on the trust that what is purchased is delivered. In his description of "trust markets," Winston cites examples of donations made to public radio (was the money really used to support programming?) and CARE packages sent to aid foreign countries (did the package really get into the hands of Somalians?) to demonstrate how much trust is invested in nonprofits when something is "purchased." The same, he says, can be said for higher education and its relationship with prospective students, the parents of those students, and other key stakeholders such as alumni and the public. "People investing in human capital through a purchase of higher education don't know what they're buying—and won't and can't know what they have bought until it is far too late to do anything about it" (Winston, 1999, p. 15). Because education is typically a "one-shot investment expenditure" (Winston, 1999, p. 15) rather than a repetitive one, it is critical that higher education make good on what it promises those who invest in it.

Colleges and universities, then, must affirm that trust by effectively communicating who they are and what they do as they offer evidence to support their claims. Complicating this effort is the student's participation. As Winston (1999) observes, students are both the customer and an input that affects the quality of the product. It is a strange kind of economics that colleges and universities must negotiate as they seek to refine and promote their identity, advance their own prestige, and attract like-minded students. Institutional prestige relies on high-quality inputs (test scores, performance, success after graduation) from the very people who are purchasing the product, changing the usual buyer-seller relationship. Rather than selling to any willing and able buyer, colleges and universities have a vested interest to ensure that who buys from them is a person they want integrated into their largest input pool. In other words, not only does a school have to get your attention and attract you to apply, it has to then determine your worthiness and support you through your time on campus so that you can positively contribute to the environment that attracted you to the institution in the first place.

This strange economy leads Winston (1999) to caution that "the standard economic intuition and analogies, built on an understanding of profit-making firms and the economic theory that supports it, are likely to be a poor guide to understanding higher education and to making predictions" (p. 33). This caution is amplified when Winston concludes that applying the economics of for-profit business to higher education does not just obscure the higher education landscape but can also "seriously distort" understanding it and appreciating its unique complexities.

Elaboration Likelihood Model

Up to this point we have seen how a person often navigates the college choice process, and we have examined the variables that contribute to decision making. To help explain the choice process as it relates to persuasion and advertising, a model of persuasion is offered here. Although numerous theories try to explain the role of persuasion in advertising (see also Agres, Edell, and Dubitsky, 1990; Perloff, 2003; Petty, Ostrom, and Brock, 1981; Silvia, 2006), this discussion is limited to a presentation of the classic dual-processing Elaboration Likelihood Model (Petty and Cacioppo, 1981, 1984a, 1984b, 1986a, 1986b) and how it explains the behavior of college and university marketing units regarding their marketing and advertising efforts.

The Elaboration Likelihood Model is a dual-process model in that it claims there are two processes by which communication influences attitude: a central route and a peripheral route. *Elaboration* refers to the extent the receiver modifies his or her thoughts on the message (does a person give the message more thought?), and *likelihood* refers to the probability that elaboration is likely or unlikely. Petty and Cacioppo (1981) describe elaboration along a continuum, with considerable rumination on the central merits of an issue at one end and relatively little mental thought about the issue on the other end. The model attempts to explain situations that are likely to make people elaborate or not elaborate on a particular issue or message.

Petty and Cacioppo's Elaboration Likelihood Model (1981) notes two distinct ways people process information. First is the central route, characterized by a clear, direct, and uncluttered message. This route is characterized by considerable cognitive elaboration and occurs when individuals focus on the central features of the message, issue, or idea. Applied to a product, one could think of the central route as being applied to the purchase of a new car in which the consumer carefully considers product qualities such as gas mileage, seating capacity, and price. As people process information centrally, they carefully evaluate the product, consider the message, and question their own needs and values as they evaluate the needs and values of the communicator. Much thought is involved with this route, which requires a strong and clear central message.

By contrast, the second route for processing a message is the peripheral route. Rather than thoughtfully considering the central message and the information presented, the peripheral route involves a quick examination of the product and a focus on simple cues about whether or not to cognitively elaborate on the message and accept or reject it. In this mode, peripheral messages are the dominate communication device for persuasion. Music playing in the background, sex appeal, a communicator's persuasive style, or just the pleasant association of the message and some nonrelated quality can translate into action. In the peripheral route, people often rely on simple rules to govern their thinking. For example, "Honda always makes quality products" or "He's the expert; I should believe what he says" or "I should do what Michael Jordon would do; he's the best basketball player ever."

Beyond the actual processing of a message, either through the central or peripheral routes, is the motivation and ability to process it, classified by the Elaboration Likelihood Model as the level of personal involvement. With the sheer volume of messages a person receives every day, it would be impossible for him or her to thoughtfully process each one. Therefore, they superficially process information until they are confronted with a message in which they are motivated to engage more thoughtfully. The motivation to process the image is characterized by low involvement (little involvement with the product, little interest in the issue) to high involvement (a high degree of personal experience or high degree of personal interest or involvement). The theory holds that if a person has a high involvement with the message, he or she should engage with it through a central route of communication and be motivated to take action (that is, receive the message or purchase the item). In the peripheral route, the person's motivation follows a different line of cognitive response. Because they are not motivated by high involvement and the central route messaging that follows it, people are likely to be persuaded to greater message elaboration when the peripheral route presents something designed to capture their attention. In conventional advertising, this phenomenon explains a half-naked Paris Hilton selling hamburgers and why attention-getting humor works well in a thirty-second spot during the Super Bowl.

When applied to higher education, this peripheral route messaging helps explain why colleges and universities often advertise and highlight elements of the college experience that have little to do with the process of learning itself. The appeal is peripheral, not central, because the central route or message is too similar across institutions. Higher education is full of similar institutions, all searching for ways to stand out from the competition. Market differentiation becomes increasingly challenging, which leads to highlighting peripheral differences, as they seem to be where the difference itself lies.

The Elaboration Likelihood Model proposes that given the lack of (strength of) a key central proposition to elaborate upon, a person may still be persuaded to take action (that is, make a choice or purchase) based on peripheral factors that are not central to a message such as attractiveness. In the especially clutter-ridden communication environments—like the ones faced by today's fragmented media audiences—such peripheral factors could help communicators achieve awareness and perhaps even arouse interest and action.

When viewed through this lens, it becomes clear that most colleges and universities lack a clear central message that allows for direct message advertising. Several factors contribute to this situation, including difficulty with market differentiation, marketing a largely intangible product, and having to rely on emotional connections and brand communities for customer loyalties. Most colleges and universities offer similar central features (similar curricula, similar housing, and so forth) in their respective institutional classifications. Thus they rely on peripheral characteristics and an emotional response from the audiences they are trying to persuade to take action on their message.

People generally process information in one of two ways: they carefully consider the message arguments, or they superficially examine the information and focus on simple facts or cues. Of chief concern for advertisers is identifying what in the act of message processing effectively persuades a person to take action in support of the product being advertised. Cognitive Response Theory (Greenwald, 1968) attempts to explain this process. A cognitive response is a thought in response to a persuasive message (Greenwald, 1968; Petty and Cacioppo, 1981). Cognitive Response Theory states that a person's own mental thoughts regarding a message are as important as the persuasion (Brock, 1967; Greenwald, 1968; Petty, Ostrom, and Brock, 1981). When people receive a message, they assess its accuracy and relevance according to preconceived ideas and experiences they have regarding the subject of the message. Cognitive Response Theory attempts to explain the attitudinal changes that occur from the time a message is received until a person takes action on the information, by either accepting or rejecting it.

Much has been written on Cognitive Response Theory and the research conducted to explore it empirically (a good place to start researching the topic is *Cognitive Responses in Persuasion* edited by Petty, Ostrom, and Brock [1981] or the works of Anthony G. Greenwald). For the purposes of this discussion, Wright's finding (1980) from several experiments in cognitive response is most informative. Based on his research, Wright found that the cognitive responses that consumers usually rely on are primarily based on their own mental images and personal experiences rather than the content of the advertisement itself. This finding has significant implications for higher education and how it markets and advertises itself. Lacking a strong central message as a point of differentiation, colleges and universities advertise many of the differences that do exist in an attempt to build positive mental images of their institution and to reinforce these images through personal contact or other tangible evidence.

College choice is a high-involvement activity that relies on preconceived images and impressions of individual institutions as much as on the substantive characteristics that exist but are difficult to communicate. Perception then becomes as important as reality. This distinction between higher education and much of the business world, which relies on reality and the tangibility of that reality to arrive at conclusions about quality, value, and satisfaction, is significant. Although temptation to use business marketing strategies, theories, and techniques and apply them to higher education is significant, differences persist that necessitate nuanced marketing approaches and actions.

Higher education is full of similar institutions, all desperate to stand out in a positive and meaningful way. Market differentiation becomes increasingly challenging, which leads to the highlighting of peripheral differences as they seem to be where difference itself lies. Colleges and universities are reduced to boasting of their multimillion-dollar student recreation centers, their nouveau chic dining residence halls, and their active participation in the academic arms race for national attention and success. Schools advertise elements of campus life that have nothing to do with academics, just to stand out. The peripheral messaging leads to ads bragging about a recreation center that is home to "the tallest climbing wall in Texas!" (University of Texas at San Antonio) or "a 53-person hot tub. The largest on any campus anywhere!" (Washington State University). The lack of central messaging also sheds light onto administrative decisions to participate in publicity media events such as hosting rocker Tommy Lee on campus for a reality TV show ("Tommy Lee Goes to College" broadcast on NBC and hosted by the University of Nebraska) as well as gimmicks designed to draw attention (Duke University's giving away iPods as "educational tools" in 2003 to much fanfare).

All these decisions and actions reflect a market (higher education) that is desperate to stand out despite the crowd. Achieving market differentiation becomes the most challenging aspect of marketing and advertising higher education. The Elaboration Likelihood Model's dual process helps to simplify how general communication occurs between businesses and their audiences and it is referred to, directly or indirectly, throughout this monograph.

This chapter presented two critical elements in the selling of higher education: persuading someone that something you have is worth purchasing and the process he or she goes through as they seek to buy it, from you or from one of your competitors. As we saw, how one goes about choosing a college to attend is a complicated process that depends on multiple informational inputs such as opinions from peers and parents and the amount of available information on different schools as well as constraining factors such as one's ability to pay for college and campus location. This process is made all the more complicated by the "trust economy" (Winston, 1999), which demands that colleges and universities effectively communicate who they are and what they do to those who invest in them. As seen through the lens of the Elaboration Likelihood Model, colleges' and universities' marketing and advertising efforts should be targeted to engage prospective students in the choice process and to create opportunities for prospective students to elaborate on the institutional message offered.

Marketing and Advertising Higher Education

THIS CHAPTER EXAMINES THE TRANSFORMATION of the marketing and advertising of higher education over the past forty years. In that time, marketing efforts at many higher education institutions have become highly organized and tightly controlled by entirely new marketing units that have been established to create, maintain, and promote a school's image. Decreases in financial support and increases in competition from for-profit institutions and others have changed the very marketplace of higher education. Scholars point to a shift in higher education as a social institution to one of industry, and they are often critical of the change. Although this shift has been derisively labeled the "commercialization" of higher education, this chapter suggests that higher education leadership can use marketing efforts to better align organization goals, be more responsive to key stakeholder needs, and be adaptive rather than prescriptive to negotiate the community's changing needs and expectations.

Brief History

Although the history in this area extends back to the earliest recruiting efforts for students, the scope of this monograph is much narrower. The intent here is to capture the major changes in the higher education marketing and advertising landscape over the past four decades and to focus more precisely on current—and future—practices and activities.

A combination of factors over the past forty years has contributed to colleges' and universities' being run more like businesses than social and educational institutions (see Bok, 2003; Kirp, 2003; Slaughter and Leslie, 1997). State and federal support of education was given a significant boost for teaching and research following the space race of the 1950s and 1960s. Congress generously funded many capital campaigns on campuses across the country, and research dollars flowed to the places likely to advance technology and scientific discoveries for the benefit of the state and private business (Bok, 2003; Zemsky, Wegner, and Massy, 2005).

Unfortunately for higher education, this level of support was short-lived; the dramatic increases in state and federal support seen through the 1950s and 1960s began to decline in the early 1970s. With an energy crisis gripping the country and more expensive demands put on the federal government to finance a costly war, Congress could not continue to support research and growth in higher education as it had in the previous two decades (Bok, 2003; Zemsky, Wegner, and Massy, 2005).

Coupled with the loss of federal support was a reduction in state-level funding of higher education. The 1980s and 1990s brought increased demands to state budgets for things like greater support of state-financed health care, increasing costs for prison construction and maintenance, and rising costs of welfare (Slaughter and Leslie, 1997).

As a result, colleges and universities were faced with a triple threat to their viability: the "great wave of public investments in higher education that had more than doubled the enterprise's capacity, largely through the creation of new campuses, had spent itself" (Zemsky, Wegner, and Massy, 2005, p. 17), the number of students was declining, and the economy was experiencing rapid inflation with stagnant outputs that, combined, raised unemployment and applied pressure to the country's already thin resources (Bok, 2003; Zemsky, Wegner, and Massy, 2005).

Faced with declining appropriations over the past thirty years, colleges and universities retooled the way they did business, and a new kind of higher education began to emerge. One could loosely think of this period as the commercialization of the modern university (Bok, 2003). Bok (2003) believes this commercialization can be attributed to a number of causes. Financial cutbacks motivated some universities to pursue profit-seeking ventures. These efforts were aided when Congress passed the Bayh-Dole Act in 1980, "which made it easier for universities to own and license patents on discoveries made through research paid for with public funds" (p. 11). Passage of this bill legitimized partnerships between the commercial interests of business and the research interests of the university. In addition to contributing to the public good, discoveries and patents opened new revenue streams to college and university administrators eager to plug budget gaps. The combination of the Bayh-Dole Act and the enthusiasm for entrepreneurial private enterprise encouraged and legitimized research for profit in higher education. Increased competition for resources and students drove institutions to reach deeper into common commercial and business practices as they realigned their priorities and started to act like the revenue centers they truly were.

Competition from For-Profit Higher Education

Throughout the 1980s and 1990s—and about the same time colleges and universities began to see a shift in their institutional missions concerning their entrepreneurial activities—a more technologically sophisticated and knowledge-based economy emerged to support their efforts to commodify their research discoveries and become more adaptive to business interests and partnerships (Bok, 2003; Kinser, 2006; Zemsky, Wegner, and Massy, 2005).

This right-place, right-time opportunity greatly benefited traditional colleges and universities, but it also opened the door for increased competition from the for-profit commercial education sector. The burgeoning online platform made it possible for organizations such as the University of Phoenix, American InterContinental University, and DeVry University to become legitimate competitors for many colleges and universities. These for-profit institutions now account for approximately 8 percent of student enrollment in colleges eligible for financial aid. Today most of the roughly 908 for-profit institutions are able to offer online courses that promise to deliver higher education to students where they are and when they need it (Foster and Carnevale, 2007).

According to Eduventures, an education consulting company, for-profit degree-granting institutions enrolled 5.1 percent of students in 2004, accounting for 37 percent of all online students (Foster and Carnevale, 2007). Currently, the University of Phoenix, which is the largest online higher education provider, has an online enrollment of almost 130,000 students (Foster and Carnevale, 2007; Rhoades, 2006).

For-profit institutions like the University of Phoenix and DeVry University can compete against taxpayer-subsidized public colleges and universities by meeting a need those schools have not. Chiefly they offer specialized programs with classes that meet in the evening or on weekends at convenient times or classes that are strictly online. The convenience of this delivery method is especially attractive for nontraditional students with families and working professionals. In addition to being convenient, they are often cheaper than state and private schools and their delivery models are truly geared toward customer satisfaction. Coupled with the convenience, Kinser (2006) rightly points out, the for-profit sector enrolls relatively higher proportions of low-income and minority students and more women, which has an impact on overall student diversity and changes the way in which degree-granting institutions might alter their advertising and marketing efforts.

For-profit institutions have taken the lead in providing online education to students both near and far. Commercial education was the first to provide online courses that students could take in the evenings, on weekends, or at any time that fit their schedules. Although online delivery of courses precludes face-to-face meeting and direct interaction between students and professors, it does provide virtual classrooms and chat environments, and it makes it relatively easy to communicate with instructors using e-mail or bulletin boards.

These commercial higher education providers offer specialized training in particular areas, they offer degrees, including advanced degrees, and they offer certification for select areas and professions. The convenience of commercial education is difficult for traditional colleges and universities to match. Although a traditional college or university degree may be regarded with more esteem (and promises a higher-quality educational experience), many students (and their employers) are not concerned—they simply want a degree.

The success of the for-profits in a highly competitive market demonstrates that commercial higher education providers are filling a niche market and satisfying consumer demands. The market has rewarded the University of

Phoenix and DeVry University for their business model, but it has also responded to something critically important for how higher education behaves in the new market economy. Commercial higher education's profitability depends largely on the staggering amount each institution spends on marketing and advertising. According to statistics provided to *The Chronicle of Higher Education*, the Apollo Group, the parent company of the University of Phoenix, spent more than $142 million on Internet advertising in a twelve-month period from September 2005 to September 2006. That amount places it among the biggest spenders for all Internet advertising, including the likes of Ford and General Motors (Blumenstyk, 2006). This heavy spending reflects an industry where institutions spend around 20 percent of their annual budgets on marketing and marketing-related activities. By comparison, nonprofit higher education spends less than 5 percent, although this figure is speculative based on expert opinion in the absence of firm numbers (Strout, 2006). In addition to all that spending, the University of Phoenix employs a call center that staffs approximately four thousand employees whose sole purpose is to contact prospects and encourage enrollment (Blumenstyk, 2006).

The lesson to be learned from the for-profit education sector is that marketing and advertising pay. It may not lead to a better product or a better experience for the consumer, but it does lead to better awareness and usually great purchasing volume. Online higher education providers employ sophisticated marketing techniques, they are doggedly determined, and they have a financial commitment to making their model work. These attributes make competing with those online providers difficult, but it provides valuable lessons for the way in which traditional colleges and universities market and advertise themselves.

The Changing Marketplace

The declining enrollments of the 1990s combined with continued decreases in state and federal funding for (public) higher education and the increasing competition from for-profit higher education "contributed to the need for many institutions of higher education to create and maintain a distinct image (a niche) in the marketplace" in an effort to position or reposition themselves (Parameswaran and Glowacka, 1995, p. 41). Less funding, fewer students, and

increased competition from for-profit education tightened the higher education market. When faced with increased competition, businesses of any kind
(including higher education) must be responsive to competitors and the needs
of the market as they assess their overall position. In higher education, and in
other businesses as well, competition brings a greater awareness of the need to
"create, disseminate, and maintain a rather distinctive image" as a means
to maintaining a competitive advantage (Parameswaran and Glowacka, 1995,
p. 42). The increasingly competitive higher education market, which began
decades ago and continues today, has more recently pushed colleges and universities to evaluate their identity and their image, establish what their
strengths and weakness are, and develop a clear mission and vision that reflects
organizational identity and aspiration as colleges and universities develop
strategies for positioning or repositioning themselves (Bok, 2003; Kirp, 2003;
Zemsky, Wegner, and Massy, 2005).

These organizational identity issues have been present in higher education
since at least the beginning of the twentieth century, and they are not new
concepts to administrators and others charged with institutional governance.
The higher education marketplace, however, has seen a dramatic shift in the
past forty years toward bringing these images and marketing practices to
the forefront with arguably the most significant external threat coming from
for-profit higher education. The emergence of online education placed outside market pressure on colleges and universities and forced them to respond
or risk losing students. Before the 1990s, distance education served a very
narrow marketing niche; today that niche is much broader and, for some institutions, represents a significant threat. Online education spends significant
amounts on marketing and advertising, and it works at a dogged pace to
siphon off students from traditional schools, both large and small (Foster and
Carnevale, 2007; Rhoades, 2006).

The change in market strategy for higher education has led many critics
to lambaste higher education for its "commercialized" approach to recruiting
and educating students (see Hayes and Wynyard, 2002; Thacker, 2005). The
term "commercialized admissions" has been used for some time now to reflect
the competitive student recruiting practices of the admissions process that
(critics argue) places more value on positioning the institution and skimming

the best students from the applicant pool and far less value on personal contact, ensuring a good fit, and delivering a quality education from admission to graduation (Thacker, 2005). This criticism has expanded to include notions of commercialized academics, not just admissions, with schools suddenly positioned as businesses selling products, offering services, and operating like corporations rather than the social institutions they have historically been.

The conflict about how to regard the modern college or university is very real, and critics' observations are astute. Strategic marketing, planning, and advertising open an institution to operations that resemble corporate America more than schooling as normal. Gumport (2000) observes that a shift of higher education from a social institution to higher education as an industry has occurred; she believes "three interrelated mechanisms have converged to advance this process" (p. 67). Primarily, she cites "the rise of academic management in colleges and universities," the rise of "academic consumerism," and "the re-stratification of academic subjects and academic personnel, based upon the increased use-value and exchange-value of particular knowledge in the wider society" (pp. 67–69). This shift in higher education from social institution to industry threatens to undermine its legitimacy as institutions move away from their "historic character, functions, and accumulated heritage as educational institutions" (p. 67) toward a pure business model. Gumport concludes by reminding the reader that research and teaching of higher education is a "public investment" and that it is precisely that public investment that defines its legacy.

Despite these truisms, traditional higher education values and practices are under intense pressure to be more accountable for who they are, what they do, and what they produce. Student enrollment, retention, and academic performance are all forcing colleges and universities to operate in a manner that is more commercial. These political and business realities are at the core of the modern higher education institution, and they must be navigated, not ignored or dismissed.

The Education Conservancy, a nonprofit group committed to reforming college admissions, advances a core set of values that are meant to buttress the commercialized nature of admissions (and academics writ large). Although longer on principle than practice, the core mission of the Conservancy in protecting traditional academic values is to regard education as "a process, not a product" and to remember that students are "learners, not customers." Further, the Conservancy suggests these educational values are best served "by admissions processes that are consistent with those values—that treat the thoughts, ideas, and passions of students as worthy of engaging" (Thacker, 2005, p. B26).

The world the Conservancy envisions is possible, but it requires strong leadership that is mindful of the market but academic at heart. Colleges and universities can successfully market themselves while adhering to education values, but doing so demands these institutions use their marketing as a way of tightening their mission, purpose, and practice. Rather than regarding marketing and advertising as some kind of "other" in the business process or running an institution, how might it instead be used as a tool to also improve identity, engage students, and better connect to the community?

Krachenberg (1972), in writing one of the first comprehensive articles on marketing of higher education, acknowledges the often negative view many people have of marketing. "It has become a catchword standing for all the undesirable elements in American business," he writes. "In short, marketing is looked upon by many as being fundamentally self-seeking and thus unacceptable by its very nature." In its true meaning, however, marketing "deals with the concept of uncovering specific needs, satisfying those needs by the development of appropriate good and services, letting people know of their availability, and offering them at appropriate prices, at the right time and place" (p. 380).

Krachenberg (1972) rightly points out that marketing itself serves a basic service to society. Marketing helps organizations identify needs, develop products and services to address those needs, and puts those goods and services into the hands of people in need. When seen in this context, marketing is a dynamic process that is responsive and innovative and not merely the symbol of all that is undesirable about business. "If anything is undesirable about marketing it is not in the activity per se; rather it is in the motives of those guiding the activity and the manner in which it is carried out" (Krachenberg, 1972, p. 380).

The business of marketing higher education need not be antithetical to good education practice. It should rather be regarded as part of the institution's educational mission. True marketing is integrated into every facet of an institution and should not be mistaken for branding or advertising (though those elements can be part of a comprehensive marketing plan) (Hesel, 2004; Neustadt, 1994; Newman, 2002). It involves intense research, usually costing $100,000 or more, to measure people's perceptions of a college, its strengths and weaknesses, and what makes it different from other institutions that are vying for the same faculty members, students, and donations (Blumenstyk, 2006). In the best scenarios, a marketing plan is formulated in conjunction with an institution's strategic plan, allowing everybody to communicate the same messages and have a clear sense of the institution's goals and values (Hesel, 2004), from both a marketing and an education perspective.

This concept dovetails with writing by Toma, Dubrow, and Hartley (2005) that identifies strong institutional culture as key to strengthening institutional identification. They persuasively argue that strong institutional identification—reinforced by clear and decisive leadership, effective external relations, and a rich campus community—extends beyond the organization and positively affects larger communities of influence. Further, strong institutional identification extends the organization beyond being "a near-inscrutable entity governed by its own mysterious sense of self" (Kellogg Commission on the Future of State and Land-Grant Institutions, 1999, p. 20) and creates a more tangible identity that is clear in purpose, thoughtfully developed, and well maintained.

For any college or university to effectively create this strong institutional identity, a strategic marketing plan should be considered a critical component of the organization's academic mission (Hesel, 2004; Keller, 1983). Likewise, the organization must know its market audience and how to appeal to it. Ongoing and successful strategic planning for organizational improvement demands knowing the product and the market. Although many in higher education are loath to reduce a college education to the status of a product, successful marketing looks objectively at a product and makes business decisions based on an honest evaluation. Good marketing knows the product, it understands the price structure, and it understands how to appeal to consumers based on what is for sale (Kotler, 1999; Kotler and Fox, 1995). Good marketing is well researched, highly coordinated, and professionally delivered (McCarthy, 1960).

The new market realities of the twenty-first-century education marketplace require responsive business practice. New market threats must be identified, acknowledged, and negotiated (Kotler and Fox, 1995). Declining enrollments, decreased state support, increased costs, and increased competition for students are realities that have led to greater academic commercialization and increased pressure on institutions to develop marketing plans and business models. The competition for students and dollars is real and so too must be the response. Resources in higher education are always scarce; tight budgets and increased scrutiny require that every dollar be spent wisely and with the greatest chance for maximized return.

The challenge is to recontextualize these business encroachments as opportunity. In many ways the intrusion of online higher education has forced mainstream colleges and universities to reevaluate who they are and articulate why they matter (Foster and Carnevale, 2007; Rhoades, 2006). They have been forced to express what makes their product superior and worth the additional cost. Traditional higher education has redoubled its efforts regarding institutional image, purpose, and vision. Increased competition between online higher education and traditional higher education and between colleges and universities themselves necessitates a clear sense of institutional identity that is well and effectively communicated to various constituencies. Recruitment and retention are essential but costly—and ever truer with more institutional options. Likewise, a clearly articulated vision and identity, one that is professionally designed and delivered, increases the likelihood that a school will stand out in a crowded marketplace (Bok, 2003; Kirp, 2003; Zemsky, Wegner, and Massy, 2005).

Understanding that marketing and advertising any product or service require thoughtful execution is a step toward working in the new marketplace of higher education. Acknowledging that higher education is "for sale" like never before does not mean surrendering all educational value and abandoning the higher education legacy Gumport describes. Higher learning does not have to be extinct as a social institution to make way for "commercialized" practice. Employing marketing techniques and strategy to improve and promote institutional identity to key stakeholders can benefit the institution in many ways. Chiefly, it can help an institution share the work it is doing with regard to educational values and practices and use that promotion as a tool for engagement with prospective students, current students, and the community.

Increased market awareness can help colleges and universities be more responsive to their community and their individual needs. Instead of opening the doors and saying, "This is what we do. We do what *we* think is best for you at times and in places that work best for us," colleges and universities should see what needs exist and how they can satisfy them. Being adaptive rather than prescriptive is how best to negotiate a changing market with changing needs and expectations.

Higher education is not industry, but it is susceptible to deeper encroachment by business, especially as marketing and advertising practices are concerned. At its core, the research and teaching of higher education are a "public investment," and they should remain that way, regardless of changing business or marketing practice. Colleges and universities need to remain social, research, and educational institutions, but they must be permitted to do so by a public that acknowledges the changing market realities of modern higher education.

Given these factors, higher education administrators must be aware of the shift that has occurred in the past forty years and not let the business side of education consume its social function and value. The new market has become largely commercialized, but all is not lost. Unlike online higher education, traditional colleges and universities dedicate themselves to education *and* research, and we depend on them to continue in that capacity. Higher education's function is critical, and individual institutions and those who govern them must take care to maintain their social function as they navigate the business realities of today.

In response to the commercialized nature of admissions and academics, most colleges and universities have established marketing departments and have hired professional directors to head them (Bok, 2003; Kirp, 2003; Pulley, 2003). Outside marketing firms are being retained to conduct market analyses, develop materials, and implement new (and often costly) marketing and advertising campaigns (Hesel, 2004; Jugenheimer, 1995; Pulley, 2003). These actions have resulted in many marketing efforts that are quite expensive and that "until now would have been unthinkable" (Pulley, 2003, p. A30). Given the money invested in modern college and university marketing and advertising, administrators with vision about how marketing the institution will reflect its actual identity and lead to expected outcomes should lead institutional efforts. A leader must champion the marketing department's efforts to assuage fears that the college or university is losing focus or forgetting the educational mission that is the foundation to everything about the institution (Newman, 2002).

This chapter examined the transformation of marketing and advertising of higher education over the past forty years. In that time, marketing efforts at many higher education institutions became highly organized and tightly controlled by entirely new marketing units that were established to create, maintain, and promote a school's image. Decreases in financial support and increases in competition from for-profit institutions and others changed the very marketplace of higher education. A review of the literature reveals that some scholars point to a shift in higher education as a social institution to one of industry, and many are critical of the change. Although that shift has been derisively labeled the "commercialization" of higher education, this chapter suggested that higher education leadership can use marketing efforts to better align organizational goals, be more responsive to key stakeholder needs, and be adaptive rather than prescriptive to negotiate the community's changing needs and expectations.

Marketing and Advertising the Intangible

THIS CHAPTER DISCUSSES THE DIFFICULTIES that accompany marketing an intangible product such as higher education and suggests that the practice of "branding" is critical to image construction. Branding creates a clear message about an intangible product and helps to build awareness and relevance in an often crowded marketplace. Branding is most successful when it involves many facets of marketing such as use of slogans and logo design but also when it is consistently maintained across the organization and provides a common image that brand communities can attach themselves to as an expression of their loyalty. A clear brand image functions as a relationship builder between individual members of the community and further binds them to the institution, both as individuals but also as separate communities that share the institution in common.

Among the greatest challenges to successfully marketing higher education is the inherently intangible nature of the very thing that is being marketed (Canterbury, 1999; Johnson and Sallee, 1994). Education is an intangible product that largely depends on a diploma as the only tangible evidence of the lived experience and learning that occurred—which is not to suggest that there are no tangible characteristics of a college or university. Finding and marketing them, however, requires more creativity than marketing a widget that people can plainly see, evaluate, and use.

The challenge of marketing an intangible product is compounded for colleges and universities because of the crowded marketplace of higher education.

Many institutions compete for everyone's attention, and they do so with things that are difficult to quantify. The primary marketing goal for colleges and universities is therefore twofold: make the intangible tangible, and find areas of market differentiation. Although both concepts—tangibility and market differentiation—are discussed in greater detail later, it is important to establish briefly that they play critical roles in general higher education marketing practice.

When considering the intangible nature of education, marketing researchers (see, for example, Johnson and Sallee, 1994: Kotler and Armstrong, 1996) suggest asking what evidence you can offer that reflects who you are and what you do as an institution. The key here is *evidence*. What can you point to and say, "See that? *That* is what we do?" Because the "results of education, such as knowledge, values, ethics, and skills are hard to conceptualize . . . admissions professionals must find and supply tangible evidence that successfully distinguishes their institution from all others" (Johnson and Sallee, 1994, p. 16). Colleges and universities generally achieve tangibility in three major areas: academics (which helps explain why rankings are so valued, even though they do not have much value), amenities and perceived social life (campus as "Club Med"), and athletics (despite the fact that a winning team bears little on the educational experience a student is likely to have). Listing these three categories is not to imply that they are the only things tangible in higher education, but much of what does become tangible in the minds of consumers can be generally placed there.

Like the challenges of marketing the intangible, successful market differentiation (standing out from your competitors) requires critical self-evaluation and creative thinking and planning. Johnson and Sallee (1994) maintain that although differentiation in the higher education marketplace is difficult at times, it can and does occur. The key is articulating product differences and characteristics and making them tangible and real in consumers' minds.

The challenge for colleges and universities is that they have to compete not only in their peer group but also with other institutions of different type. For example, small private institutions compete among themselves, but they also compete with big state schools.

Images of Colleges and Universities

Advertise an image, not a product [Pendergrast, 2000, p. 463].

When Canon introduced the advertising campaign "Image is everything" and cast tennis sensation Andre Agassi as its pitchman, it entered into what could be described as near perfect "triple-entendre marketing" that was heavy on symbolism and subtle on irony. "Image is everything" was the perfect slogan: it spoke to the quality of photographs a Canon camera was likely to produce, it was spoken by a tennis star who (at that time) was at the top of his game and well known for his style and image (both in his play and dress), and it spoke to the brand-name cache of Canon as a top manufacturer of quality photographic equipment. To be seen shooting a Canon elevated the status of the consumer whose image was presumably enhanced by his good judgment when purchasing a camera. For Canon, for Agassi, and for the consumer who responded favorably to the ad, image was everything.

Image is not everything for colleges and universities, but it is close. The image people have of an institution influences so many of the decisions they will make and the actions they will take as a result of that image. When a person is asked about your institution, what is the primary image that comes to mind? How much control over that image do you think you have, and how best do you change that image should you elect to?

A positive college or university image is a valuable asset in a competitive marketplace. Likewise, a negative image can create barriers that constantly require negotiating. Institutional image, "however formed, and based in fact or fiction," influences so much about a university's future (Landrum, Turrisi, and Harless, 1998, p. 53). Not only does it influence whether or not prospective students will enroll but also whether or not those who have enrolled stay or leave. Institutional image affects the community's attitude, both locally and statewide. A positive image is more likely to translate to greater state support and private donations. An institution that is positively regarded is more likely to endear itself to alumni and supporters. In short, it pays to have a positive institutional image.

In the marketing literature, the halo effect is borrowed from cognitive psychology to explain how an overall image can be derived from individual characteristics or attributes of an organization or brand (Leuthesser, Kohli, and

Harich, 1995). If one distinguishing characteristic is positive, others must be as well. In the absence of complete information, people often use "an overall 'good reputation' to fill in the missing details" (Landrum, Turrisi, and Harless, 1998, p. 55). The iPod has been used as an example of how positive perceptions of Apple products are created as a result of its success. Increased Apple computer sales following the success of the iPod is one example of the halo effect at work for different products offered by the same company.

Corporations usually do not have just one image; multiple images are projected into the marketplace, and their composite forms an overall identity (Dowling, 1988). Likewise, colleges and universities project several images to different groups, which each "see" the institution and its parts differently and judge it by characteristics that vary by proximity, relationship, and level of access (Parameswaran and Glowacka, 1995). Many characteristics shape and influence institutional image for higher education: perceived academic reputation, one's familiarity with the institution, cost, alumni employability, athletics, and others' (parents, peers, teachers, guidance counselors) opinions.

According to Fram (1982), outside constituencies compose ideas about college and university images according to perceptions of the faculty, the curriculum that is offered, the perceived quality, and the relationship between tuition and quality. An "institution's actual quality is often less important than its prestige or reputation for quality" (Fram, 1982, p. 6, as cited in Landrum, Turrisi, and Harless, 1998, p. 56). Fram observes that once an institution has established a positive image, it can provide valuable marketing for many years. If that statement is true, then the inverse is likely true as well, which holds implications for those institutions that carry a negative image they would like to change or shed. Patience likely rules the day for the reversal of a negative image. As for recommendations regarding the enhancement of institutional image, Fram suggests highlighting faculty accomplishments and achievements, monitoring current student attitudes, surveying the alumni about their satisfaction with the university experience, and researching the attitudes of the local community.

Based on a factor analysis of institutional characteristics that parents of prospective students in their study rated as important, Landrum, Turrisi, and Harless (1998) find that "strength of academic program and the appropriate emphasis on athletics are significant components of the image model.

Reputation or image then plays a significant role in the implementation or practical application of that image construct, namely, whether a person would send their son or daughter to the university" (p. 66). In other words, perceived strength of academics (a central route message) and an emphasis on athletics (a peripheral route message) form a composite image that leads to action. Collectively, these intangible characteristics form the basis for image perception and quality assessment. As Weissman (1990) observes, "Colleges and universities need to keep in mind that it is the organization's image, not necessarily its reality, that people respond to" (p. 67). Perhaps image really is everything.

Branding

> Factories rust away, packages become obsolete, products lose their relevance. But great brands live forever [Backer, Spielvogel, and Bates, 1991, p. 7].

In marketing and advertising, nothing beats a good brand. Brands enjoy instant credibility and sudden recognition (Aaker, 2000). Brands speak to more than just their product: they bring with them a known presence and an invisible privilege over other products like them. Brands have an advantage over nonbrands, and the best marketers use this advantage scrupulously. Most important, brands have power (Martin, 1989). They have the power to transcend fads and fickle markets. They have power to dominate.

Branding is not just another dimension of image (Sevier, 2001). Branding is a distinct classification of product awareness. When applied to higher education, branding is really image construction, image management, or image makeover. Branding is about asking, When a person hears our name, what does he or she think about?

Cobb-Walgren, Ruble, and Donthu (1995) write that "brand equity has emerged as one of the most critical areas for marketing management" and rhetorically ask why consumers are willing "to pay so much for brand names" (p. 25). The answer, they say, is simple: brand names add value to the product. "The added value that a brand name gives to a product is now commonly referred to as 'brand equity,'" which has become a defining feature of the product's perceived quality (Aaker, 1991, as cited in Cobb-Walgren, Ruble, and Donthu, 1995, p. 27). And empirical research indicates that brand name recognition can strongly influence consumer purchasing behavior (Aaker, 2000; Blackscon, 1992). Reliance on a well-known brand name also reduces risk for consumers when they are not familiar or lack experience with a product (Parameswaran and Glowacka, 1995). For that reason, brand equity is an important component of the marketing plan for colleges and universities.

When the principles behind brand name construction are applied to higher education, one gains an appreciation for how vital brand name recognition can be for attracting attention. Cobb-Walgren, Ruble, and Donthu (1995) demonstrate through research that similar brands, regardless of high or low financial risk, sell at different rates based on the amount of marketing dedicated to each. The brand with the "higher advertising budget yield[s] substantially higher levels of brand equity" (p. 25). Furthermore, they conclude, "the brand with the higher equity in each [financial risk] category generate[s] significantly greater preferences and purchase intentions" (p. 25). When applied to college and university marketing, the ability to "brand" the school takes on great significance that can carry over to several areas of institutional image that can elicit responses from various audiences.

Although the terms "product" and "brand" are used almost interchangeably in the daily lexicon, a clear distinction between the two exists in the marketing world. A product is "something that offers a functional benefit," whereas a brand is a "name, symbol, design, or mark that enhances the value of a product beyond its functional value" (Farquhar, 1989, p. 24). A pair of shoes is a pair of shoes is a pair of shoes, but a pair of Nike shoes is something else entirely. Nike symbolizes Michael Jordan and "Just Do It," winning, and everything else that screams thirty years of Nike advertising. Over the long term, it works as a marketing device, and the brand gains distinction over other manufacturers' products in the minds of consumers. When consumers buy Nikes, they pay for more than shoes; they pay for the perceived quality only a brand name like Nike can deliver.

Awareness and relevance are the two essential elements of a brand (Martin, 1989; Ries and Ries, 1998; Sevier, 2001). Bringing awareness to the product is the first goal of a branding campaign. Ask yourself whether, of all the commercial messages a person receives in a day, yours stands out. What can you do to make people take notice of you? This proposition is challenging in a media-saturated environment. The average person receives thousands of media messages per day, so standing out can be difficult. The good news is that your message is likely to be received by an audience more prepared for your message than the others that fly by in a blur. Prospective students are likely to be seeking you out as they consider where to attend college. Alumni have an existing relationship with you; they are not prospective customers whom you must attract with gimmicks or aggressive strategies. And potential donors are quite likely to be looking for reasons to give to your institution; your job is to convince them to do so.

Brands become stronger when the focus is narrow (Pearson, 1996), so careful planning is required to establish reasonable expectations for a new branding campaign. The goals and expectations should be clearly articulated, and they should focus on a single or fixed outcome. The goal is not to be everything to everyone. Nike is now for great athletic apparel and shoes but not for paint and automobiles. As Ries and Ries (1998) point out, brands should strive to "own" a word in the minds of consumers. When a person thinks of medicine or architecture or engineering, what do they think of? What about a liberal arts education in the Pacific Northwest? Does your school come to mind? If not, how can you change it so it does? Maybe the focus needs to be narrowed or the terms changed. Instead of trying to be *the* liberal arts college in the Pacific Northwest, the goal should be to be *the Catholic* liberal arts college in the Pacific Northwest. Believe it. Own it. Broadcast it. Live it. Make it your brand.

Building brand awareness requires patience and creativity. Creativity stands out in a crowded marketplace. Think of creative advertising that has worked on you. What are the ads you are likely to remember? Chances are they had memorable slogans or catchy music, tag lines or rhyming schemes or visuals that were nearly impossible to ignore. The characteristics that made those advertisements succeed illustrate creative marketing and advertising at work. Naturally, you cannot just go throw a catchy jingle onto a thirty-second television spot and expect the country to be humming your tune, but you should be open to new ideas and let the imagination run a bit. You cannot run the same tired ads claiming excellence and promising to deliver the leaders of tomorrow if you expect to stand out. Awareness requires something interesting.

The second half of branding is making your message relevant. Does the audience perceive your brand as something that might fill a perceived need? Does your message "make sense" for the target audience? And is the branding effort creating a relationship between the current message and previous messages that featured the brand, and is it establishing a pattern for future messages? (Martin, 1989; Sevier, 2001). Brand patterning creates relevance as the audience begins to see the whole institutional message over time and across themes. In the same way that Nike is a brand that extends far beyond sneakers, so too does an institution offer multiple products to multiple audiences. Nike is known for quality products that are cool and fashionable and aligned with personalities and values customers find appealing. Nike's brand identity forms an emotional bond with customers who derive emotional benefit from being associated with its attributes, personalities, and beliefs (Pearson, 1996). Colleges and universities should aim for that same emotional bond with prospective students, current students, alumni, boosters, and the community. Give them reasons to want to be associated with you.

The good news for colleges and universities is that institutions with strong brand identity carry a halo of positive assumptions about them (Landrum, Turrisi, and Harless, 1998), not unlike Nike does for things beyond shoes. The halo effect allows for certain facets of an institution to influence perceptions about the whole organization (Leuthesser, Kohli, and Harich, 1995). A strong veterinarian medicine program creates a positive halo that covers other departments and programs. A person might assume that because the veterinary school is strong, so too must be the rest of the organization. This observation is true for academics, but it is also true for other characteristics that make up an institution's identity, including athletics. A successful athletic department is not correlated to better academics or a richer academic experience for nonathletes, but the halo effect suggests that the perceived academic quality of an institution will sometimes enjoy a better reputation as a result of a well-known college athletic brand. (The inverse is sometimes true as well; schools with strong athletic brand names can be labeled "football schools" or "basketball schools," creating a negative halo effect—the "horns effect" or "devil's effect") (Leuthesser, Kohli, and Harich, 1995).

Other positive halos exist in addition to successful athletic programs. It is common for schools to market and advertise themselves on the strength of their medical schools (Johns Hopkins), the high number of national merit scholars they have (Fordham), or by showcasing high-profile faculty (Harvard). Tangibility is key, which helps explain the arms race with campus amenities and the judicious use of college ranks in promotional materials. A world-class student recreation center and nouveau chic student union are not necessarily tied to better learning, but they do communicate to students (and others) that a school is a desirable destination or at least offers desirable facilities.

First-class amenities, a prestigious law or medical school, and reputable faculty are just a few of the tangible features a school has at its disposal that can offer a positive halo to other parts of the campus. Recognizing and featuring those elements become critical when communicating an identity and advancing a brand, especially in a crowded field with few tangible product features. The key is to recognize the power of the halo effect and use it to your competitive marketing advantage.

As we move past the components of branding and consider the branded message that will be broadcast, a series of questions should be considered. Does your brand communicate the same core message to all constituents? Do students reflect essentially the same beliefs as people working in the organization (for example, new student services, admissions, financial aid, and housing)? Does the community regard the branded institution as it is intended to be received? And is the branded message the same one prospective students receive? Do donors and alumni feel valued and cared for in a manner consistent with your brand? Answers to these questions inform how well the message behind the brand works. Market analysis, both internal and external, allows for message evaluation and retooling as necessary. A message that does not work after rollout is not likely to work down the road either. It is much better to know that the message is not working early and retool as appropriate.

Marlboro College, a small liberal arts school in Vermont, learned the lesson about community involvement and branding the hard way. Seeking to better communicate the quirkiness of the institution, Marlboro hired an outside marketing firm to create an advertising campaign in 2000 that would communicate what makes Marlboro—and its three hundred students—distinct.

The print ads featured several current students juxtaposed against historic figures Langston Hughes, Eleanor Roosevelt, Jack Kerouac, and Janis Joplin—all dubbed "nonconformists"—who all attended the college at one time or another. The ad boasted that Marlboro attracted alternative students and was "a good fit . . . for people who don't want to fit in" (Gose, 2000, p. A50).

Many students and faculty responded negatively to the ad and circulated a petition demanding that the campaign be withdrawn. Approximately one-third of the student body and nearly half the faculty members signed the petition. Facing criticism, the administration defended the ad campaign and the school's continued use of it but conceded that students should have played a role in its creation (Gose, 2000).

Marlboro College stands as an example of both the need to include internal stakeholders (like students) in construction of the message as well as the need to take risks when pushing a new message. A fine line exists between being "just another college brochure" and bringing out a new message that attempts to stand apart from the crowd. The message is key, and artfully crafting and delivering it is not always a precise science.

As the message behind the brand is created, revised, or evaluated, Sevier (2001) reminds us that a brand is a "trustmark, a warrant, and a promise" (p. 78). Just as a brand rises above the level of a simple product, so too must the ability to deliver on those brand expectations. A college or university brand, or even just its image, must be grounded in reality: your market audiences will judge you based on their expectations, perceptions, and experiences (Aaker, 2000; Sevier, 2001), and they can be harsh critics. What they perceive and experience of your brand or your image will go a long way toward determining whether they are satisfied and likely to take action in support of your brand and institution. Risk of a negative backlash exists for those institutions that do not live up to expectations or for downright deception. Promise only what you think you can reasonably deliver, and make good on those promises that go unmet to the best of your ability. Above all else, do what is necessary to live up to the brand you have created.

Sevier (2001) recommends this seven-step branding strategy as marketing units consider how best to take their image and attempt to elevate it to brand status:

1. Identify the essential qualities your constituencies demand of you and the needs they expect you to fill.
2. Determine how well these constituencies perceive that you deliver on these expectations and whether you fulfill their needs.
3. Identify the performance and perception gaps you want to fill.
4. Respond to the information above strategically. Have a plan.
5. Revise and prioritize the essential qualities you want to communicate to your niche audiences.
6. Develop and implement a brand strategy.
7. Test and refine.

As Sevier points out, these steps are similar to the design and planning of a mission or vision statement. The intentional similarities reflect the strategic nature of branding. In many ways, the branding strategy is simply an extension of the existing mission statement and its strategic plan.

People taking action on your brand is the truest evidence of a successful branding effort (Martin, 1989; Ries and Ries, 1998). Do prospective students enroll? Do current students stay? Do institutional personnel embody the essential characteristics of the branded institution? Do alumni brag? Do donors give? In other words, do people take action to give the brand that certain something that elevates the institution from the commodity ranks to that of branded status? Are people willing to take action that reflects they are willing to pay the premium associated with your brand? The true test of a brand is whether a person will choose it even if they have to pay a premium for it. Give your audience something they will pay extra for.

The literature is replete with caution about how a brand is not built overnight (Blackscon, 1992; Martin, 1989; Pearson, 1996; Sevier, 2001). Success is measured in decades, not years (Sevier, 2001). Branding takes time and requires patience, purpose, and perseverance. Hesel (2004) advises institutions to be committed for the long term and not be tempted to switch to a new fashionable way of marketing or a new fashionable identity every few years. Branding efforts must be strategic in nature and thoughtfully executed. They should involve many players in the institution, all keeping in mind that brand is about the institution and the audience and about staying within the institution's overarching marketing goals. Branding works only when everything about the university's advertising and marketing is on point and highly coordinated. Brands can be changed—but only infrequently and only very carefully (Farquhar, 1989). Care must be taken at every stage of development, implementation, and evaluation to minimize the need for rebranding.

Advertising the Brand

So how might a university build itself into a brand? Baker (1999) analyzed affective conditioning and mere exposure advertising techniques and their potential effect on consumer brand choice. Affective conditioning and mere exposure are two processes in which "affect can be effortlessly transferred from an advertisement to a brand" (Baker, 1999, p. 31). In the case of affective conditioning, repeated pairs of "unconditional stimulus ([for example], a beautiful sunset) with a conditioned stimulus ([such as] Tylenol) can cause the conditioned stimulus (Tylenol) to automatically evoke a conditioned response (. . . the same good feeling that the beautiful sunset evokes)" (Baker, 1999, p. 31, citing Shimp, Stuart, and Engle, 1991).

The mere exposure procedure is even easier to execute: "the repeated exposure of a stimulus (Tylenol), in the absence of any other stimuli ([that is], only the name is repeated), can evoke an effective response" (Baker, 1999, p. 31, citing Bornstein, 1989; Zajonc, 1968). Mere exposure requires only repeating the brand name to the consumer over and over to build affinity and brand equity. The more Harvard University is used as the example of the best university in America, the more the general public accepts it as fact. The significance of this effect is enormous for colleges and universities that use their successful big-time college sports programs or a high *U.S. News & World Report* ranking to elevate their "product" to "brand" status. The University of Notre Dame is an excellent academic university that is well known because of its decades of success in sports. With the help of its athletic department, Notre Dame has been transformed into an iconic brand. Likewise, Yale University is a brand name with more than a century of prestigious images of academic excellent. When one hears "Yale," he or she thinks Ivy League, prestige, and academic privilege.

Absent any extraordinary circumstances, it is unlikely most institutions, particularly local and state colleges, will become household names based strictly on their research and academic accomplishments. Affective conditioning and mere exposure, however, suggest that a university can build itself into brand status (or at least closer to it) with highly visible image builders such as a successful athletic department, unrivaled campus amenities, or high academic rankings.

How much affective conditioning and mere exposure influence consumer habits is still in dispute, as some researchers question whether the observed effects on brand attitude can translate into effects on brand choice (Baker, 1999, citing Bierley and others, 1985; Shimp and others, 1991). Baker (1999) argues, however, that affective conditioning and mere exposure may have a larger effect on brand choice than on brand attitude. "The approach tendencies created by [affective conditioning] and [mere exposure] may be preattitudinal in the sense that they do not require the type of deliberate processing that is required to form brand attitudes" (Baker, 1999, p. 32, citing Krugman, 1965; Nord and Peter, 1980; Ray and others, 1973; Smith and Swinyard, 1983; Zajonc, 1968). Baker (1999) notes that the critical factor may be that affective conditioning and mere exposure affect "brand choice decisions when brands tie on tangible criteria" (p. 32).

Applying this logic, could simple name recognition through marketing and advertising efforts, whatever their form, differentiate one school from another in the minds of new students and faculty? If so, what kind of "value" does this name recognition carry? As many have said over the years when referring to unexpected good fortune and attention, You can't pay for this kind of advertising! A successful marketing program, well developed, well executed, and well promoted, might make the difference between a university offering a product and one that becomes a recognized brand. Both affective conditioning and mere exposure require heavy brand name exposure to solidify the brand name in consumers' minds, which is exactly what an aggressive marketing campaign is designed to do.

Although hitting the trifecta of successful marketing—a campaign that is well developed, well executed, and well promoted—is a tall order, some institutions have found success in completely rebranding themselves. The University of

Maryland at College Park faced a serious identity crisis in the mid-1980s when All-American basketball star Len Bias died in his dorm room of a cocaine overdose. Students began backing out of their enrollment commitments, and the school faced the daunting task of avoiding a bad, and potentially long-lasting, label and moving forward, getting across the message that the school is still a good place to attend. To confront the situation, the university began what *The Chronicle of Higher Education* says is "one of the boldest promotional campaigns ever seen in higher education" (Pulley, 2003, p. A30). Over the next twenty years, the school established a marketing office, embarked on its first major fundraising campaign, redesigned its logo and all of its promotional materials (thanks in part to professional firms it hired), and truly reinvented itself. The efforts have paid off in increased applications and donations, indicating to administrators the rebranding effort has worked (Pulley, 2003).

Brand Communities

Although the thought of branding a college or university offends many academicians, who would prefer that higher education remain higher education (Bok, 2003; Kirp, 2003; Zemsky, Wegner, and Massy, 2005), branding works particularly well for colleges and universities because of the importance of brand communities and the positive impact they can have on an organization. Current research into brand communities (McAlexander, Koenig, and Schouten, 2004; McAlexander, Schouten, and Koenig 2002; Muniz and O'Guinn, 2001) reveals their importance, "which [consists] of all the people for whom a particular brand is relevant and the relationships they form in the context of using the brand" (McAlexander, Koenig, and Schouten, 2004, p. 62). In this research, a common theme emerged from the findings: "loyalty to the brand is a function of integration in the brand community, [that is], of more and stronger relationships binding a person to the community" (McAlexander, Koenig, and Schouten, 2004, p. 62).

As McAlexander, Koenig, and Schouten (2004) observe, a college or university is a brand community with a broad assortment of entities and a number of relationships between them. Members include (but are not limited to) "students, parents, alumni, faculty and staff, landlords, merchants, sports fans, and other members of the surrounding towns and neighborhoods" (p. 63). To this list I would add state and regional communities and legislators as well as donors, both large and small. And for institutions that feature national sports programs, national-level donors, athletic boosters, and sports fans who may have no connection to the institution except through the support of sports teams all become part of that branded community.

These entities form relationships with each other "but also with the university as a marketing organization and as the owner and steward of a brand as manifest in logos, mascots, athletic teams, and other icons" (p. 64). This brand community gives common purpose and a central route for communication between colleges and universities and their various stakeholders and audiences. Brand communities maintain the brand just as the marketers behind the brand have the power to shape the brand and potentially the brand community. "Whether unintentionally, or by design, marketers play a part in shaping and maintaining brand communities. University administrators may benefit from identifying means to foster a healthy brand community and, thereby, to impact important marketing outcomes" (McAlexander, Koenig, and Schouten, 2004, p. 64). It is especially true as a brand gains traction among various stakeholders and the brand community sees the common purpose behind their activities and relationships.

Slogans and Logos

World Class. Face to Face. [Washington State University]
The Character of Success. [Bryant University]
Live, Learn and Thrive. [New Mexico State University]

Slogans and logos have the power to communicate a targeted message and are generally regarded as part of a branding campaign (Bauerly and Tripp, 1997; Katz and Rose, 1969; Pulley, 2003). They communicate institutional personality and in some cases are heatedly debated by students, administrators, alumni, and faculty, who all believe they know what the slogan or logo *should have been* and not what was designed.

A catchy slogan can serve a brand for years. General Electric still brings "good things to light," even though its slogan changed two years ago, and Nike has had people "Just Do[ing] It" for more than a decade. But bad labeling can often be as sticky as good. No one wants to roll out a new slogan and stamp it on every printed copy and Web site the university creates, only to bury it six months later after it has been roundly mocked.

To be memorable, one has to be noticed. But as the old adage goes, sometimes no news is better than bad news. A bad slogan is far worse than none at all. The University of Idaho unveiled a new slogan and ad campaign revolving around the slogans "No Fences" and "Open Space. Open Minds" only to be panned by the community. Enrollment actually dropped over the one-year adoption of the slogans, and students and faculty steadily resisted the new label (Bartlett, 2007).

Bauerly and Tripp (1997) believe that successful slogan development involves multiple levels of participants, "appropriate screen criteria, and a solid understanding of an institution's strengths and publics" (p. 1). A new slogan often complements new layouts, a new logo, a new name, new designs, new majors, new whatever (Bauerly and Tripp, 1997; Katz and Rose, 1969; Pulley, 2003). If a campaign is "drastically changed, then a new or modified slogan may be needed to reflect the new message strategy," (Bauerly and Tripp, 1997, p. 2).

Bauerly and Tripp (1997) point out that slogans are effective for "establishing or perpetuating a central theme or image over a lengthy period of time" (p. 2). To be truly effective, slogans should reflect the spirit of the new campaign and genuinely reflect the institution they are representing. They should also involve representatives from the whole campus community. Administrators, student services personnel, various frontline people who regularly greet the public, faculty, current students, alumni, and members of the community should all be part of the selection process.

Creating a good slogan is difficult. A slogan might be only four words, but it has to be the right four words, in the right order, with the right punctuation, or it does not work. The devil truly is in the details.

To make the job easier, Krugman, Reid, Dunn, and Barban (1994) present some general rules for writing a slogan. Slogans should:

1. Be easy to remember and not confusing.
2. Make it easy to differentiate the product from the competition.

3. Be made to provoke curiosity and thought.
4. Use rhyme or have a rhythm or use alliteration.

And they should be punchy and short. Brevity and wit are the soul of slogans. Last, slogans should be able to transcend an institution's disciplinary boundaries. No one wants to study Renaissance history at a school whose slogan is "Business is our business . . . and our only business."

Once a slogan has been adopted, caution should be exercised before rushing out to stamp it on catalogues, viewbooks, and other print and digital media (Bauerly and Tripp, 1997). It would be much better to test the slogan on a focus group comprising the target market group. Conducting a focus group allows the creative team to see whether the slogan evokes the intended response. Focus-group testing also prevents a creative "blind spot" from obscuring what is painfully obvious to audiences outside the design room. It is much better to be embarrassed through testing than public mocking.

Branding is most successful when it involves many facets of marketing such as slogans and logos but also when it is consistently maintained across the organization and provides a common image that brand communities can attach themselves to as an expression of their loyalty. A clear brand image functions as a relationship builder between individual members of the community and further binds them to the institution, as individuals but also as separate communities that share the institution. This chapter discussed the difficulties that accompany marketing an intangible product such as higher education and suggests that the practice of "branding" is critical to image construction. Branding creates a clear message about an intangible product and helps to build awareness and relevance in an often crowded marketplace, especially as colleges and universities struggle to stand out, or even be noticed, in a crowded marketplace.

Market Differentiation

THE FOCUS OF THIS CHAPTER shifts to an examination of how institutional identity and branding are essential to standing apart in a crowded marketplace. Market differentiation in higher education involves communicating how your institution best suits consumers' needs and is the best choice of the available options. Different institutions accomplish this feat differently, but it often involves communicating to multiple audiences the quality of the academic offerings, describing social and campus amenities, and, often, aligning the success of the athletic department to the rest of the institution. A professionally developed marketing plan that includes professionally designed promotional materials, viewbooks that reflect the institutional brand, and a digital presence that is geared toward communicating with a twenty-first-century audience is key to successful communication of what makes an institution stand apart from the competition.

Market Differentiation

Market differentiation is simply standing out in a crowd—making your product stand apart from others in a meaningful way. The goal is not just to look different; it is also to look more appealing so that a consumer is more likely to take action on your product instead of others that are equally available. Successful market differentiation requires articulating your product's differentiating qualities or characteristics when compared with those of your competition (Johnson and Sallee, 1994; Jugenheimer, 1995; Kotler, 1999; Martin, 1989). Market differentiation is largely about persuasion. The goal is to persuade the audience that you have a product that is both *different* and *better* than your competitor's similarly designed and marketed product. Persuading people to take action on something is not an inherently negative concept, even if it does somehow seem manipulative and deceitful. Persuasion is really about understanding how people process information as part of their cognitive thinking and how to ensure your message is part of the choice set. Market differentiation works when a message is clearly articulated, when it is carefully and purposefully delivered, and when the points of distinction between two similar products are made plain to the audience.

Differentiation in the higher education marketplace is challenging, but it can occur. "Admissions professionals have the ability to define for prospects the slight but important differences between their institution and those with which they are compared" (Johnson and Sallee, 1994, p. 18). Johnson and Sallee suggest doing so by highlighting class size, housing advantages, social life distinctions, or quality of faculty. The difficulty, of course, is that when everyone is highlighting class size, housing advantages, social life distinction, and quality of faculty, everyone suddenly looks a lot alike again.

One could argue that market differentiation in higher education is more about *perceptions* of difference than true difference. Most people do not have the kind of access to colleges and universities that would allow them to make direct comparisons on the numerous characteristics that truly make institutions different from one another. Instead, they are asked to see differences when presented with selectively highlighted information that tends to look very similar. After all, most colleges and universities, when separated by type and classified according to peer group, generally offer the same things: on the surface, they tend to have the same faculty to student ratios, they provide similar housing options, and they offer social experiences that are likely very similar.

The solution, then, lies in highlighting and advertising the minor differences that do exist but are probably not obvious to the target market audiences (such as prospective students and their parents for recruiting and donors and alumni for giving and other support). As Sharp and Dawes (2001) observe, "Real world differentiation is a pervasive feature of modern markets, but seems to be largely due to differences in distribution and awareness, and occasionally design" (p. 739). In other words, it is not that the products are substantively different; the difference lies in how to build product awareness and generate appeal that leads to action. Differentiation, then, is not simply product dependent. Products can differentiate themselves on quality and availability, but generally they are differentiated on awareness.

The marketing literature (Best, 2004; Day, 1999; Kotler, 1999; Kotler and Armstrong, 1996; Kotler and Fox, 1995; Kotler and Keller, 2006), notes elements of marketing and advertising that lead to differentiation between competing products and services. They include differences in price, position, product, quality, advertising, brand awareness, and design. It is incumbent on the persons charged with marketing and advertising an institution to consider how best to stand apart from the competition and communicate the "slight but important differences," that exist (Johnson and Sallee, 1994, p. 18).

These slight but important differences often emanate from the common differentiation features discussed in the marketing literature (Best, 2004; Day, 1999; Kotler, 1999; Kotler and Armstrong, 1996; Kotler and Fox, 1995; Kotler and Keller, 2006), which include, among other things:

Being exclusively available. Providing the only product or service at the time a customer has a need is a powerful marketing advantage. Unfortunately, this option is rarely available to institutions of higher education.

Providing a better product. A better product will lead to greater sales if customers know that differences in quality exist. Let your customers know you are better and how. Colleges and universities have several options to communicate how they "offer a better product"—highlighting campus amenities, focusing on the college community where a school resides, and promoting tangible evidence of academic success such as national merit scholars, prominent faculty, institutional rankings, and overall student achievement.

Providing better service. Better service, like a better product, leads to greater sales. Better quality service requires strong customer relations that are responsive to needs, acted on in a timely fashion, and accurate. A college that feels it offers the best support and "service" for its students as they navigate advising, financial aid, and housing would be wise to set those features prominently in front of prospective applicants. Tell students about your attentive staff and personal contact with faculty. These service features help establish how you are the better value.

Providing a better value. Because price is difficult to adjust in the short-term in higher education—and might not be possible at all—emphasizing you are a better value is much more realistic and more likely to yield greater success. Tell people why you are the best value and how they get their money's worth with you versus the competition. You both charge the same, but your graduates are better employed after graduation. That kind of distinction indicates more bang for the buck and resonates with customers looking for quality and value.

Providing a better price. Quite simply, who has the lowest price? A lower price wins out when identical products are equally available. But this option is also difficult for many colleges and universities. A better strategy is for colleges and universities to communicate why they are a better value versus a lower price than their competition.

Providing convenient access. Sometimes it all comes down to *convenience.* How convenient is the purchase, and does that convenience nullify other differences, like price? Convenient access is central to discussions of market differentiation, although it is not as applicable to colleges and universities as it is to airport snack bars and umbrella salesmen standing on the corner in a thunderstorm.

Providing personalized solutions to customers' needs. Personalized marketing has become increasingly more popular with technological advances and increased Internet use (Kittle, 2000). The ability to e-mail and text potential students regarding their college choice is just one example of this feature at work. The challenge is to make things personal without being intrusive (Kittle, 2001). Making a personal connection with a potential student has the ability to make the person feel at home and might create the subtle difference between your institution and the one down the road. Efforts should be made to personalize the college-choice process when feasible and realistic.

Market Differentiation at Work in Higher Education

Unfortunately for higher education administrators, applying the marketing principles of differentiation to the real world of academics is not easy. Colleges and universities are not like most companies that make and sell products or offer services. Colleges and universities are resistant to change, slow to implement change when it is imposed, and often do not operate with a common purpose (beyond some vague notion of their mission and purpose, both as an institution and as part of higher education in general). An English professor is not likely to give much thought to how her students are marketed to and recruited. The challenge for higher education administrators is to identify how their institution should be differentiating itself and to communicate those key differences to all members of the campus community. Further, discussing market differentiation theoretically and actually putting it to work for a college or university require patience, leadership, and vision.

Given what is known about market differentiation, how does a college or university go about differentiating itself from its competition? Market differentiation in higher education seems to occur in three general areas that enable an institution to make tangible the numerous intangible characteristics of an educational experience and provide research for myriad disciplines: (1) perceived academic quality, (2) perceived social life and campus amenities, and (3) a successful and visible athletic program. Naturally, much more contributes to a quality higher education experience, but the goal of marketing higher education is not to highlight everything good about an institution. It is to make the intangible both tangible and desirable. Becoming part of the choice set and standing out when in it are about marketing qualities people recognize as important and are likely to take action on.

Perceived Academic Quality

"College rankings!" If you think yelling "fire" in a crowded meeting of university administrators is likely to get people on their feet, try yelling "college rankings" and watch them spring to life. College rankings are a dubious measure of academic quality, to be sure, but they are about the only one available and they are popular, so people use them to market their schools and manipulate them and use them as virtually the only indicator of academic quality for higher education.

College rankings are talked about with equal parts reverence and revulsion. They attract a lot of attention, but they have been derided as "representational popularity contests" (Frederickson, 2001, p. 53), "a beauty contest" (Arnoldy, 2007, p. A6), and, in a letter written by twenty-four presidents of liberal arts colleges excoriating *U.S. News and World Report* for its rankings (Farrell and Van Der Werf, 2007, p. A11), something that "degrades the educational worth . . . of the college search process." Because they are the only available indicator of academic quality, they receive a disproportionate amount of attention from prospective students and others looking to judge the academic merits of an institution. *U.S. News and World Report* has made its college ranking guides a key feature of its business model, as it seems to have a rankings issue out every quarter and it offers supplements and books that line racks and shelves all year. (A former editor of *U.S. News and World Report* once remarked that the magazine's annual college rankings issue was for *U.S. News* what the annual swimsuit issue is for *Sports Illustrated* [Frederickson, 2001]).

U.S. News and World Report has published its ranking of the top fifty "best colleges" (four-year institutions) since 1983 and the top fifty business, law, education, medicine, and engineering graduate programs since 1990 (Dahlin-Brown, 2005). Online and in print, *U.S. News and World Report* claims to provide information on more than nineteen hundred colleges and universities, including national universities, liberal arts colleges, and schools with master's programs (www.usnews.com). Great pressure is placed on schools because they know a drop in rank could affect enrollments, future funding and research monies, and their overall reputation (Mallette, 1995).

In the world of college rankings, *U.S. News and World Report* is king, and numerous institutions advertise their rankings, often in exceptionally creative ways, to promote the most intangible (but also the most important) feature they offer: academics. It becomes the big challenge for colleges and universities: how to market and advertise the most important institutional feature that no one can see. To do so, marketers must find the tangible evidence of academic quality that is available and advertise it in the hope the audience will make the necessary connection. Rankings are far from perfect, but they are tangible. Because they are tangible, and because *U.S. News and World Report* has so aggressively sold the public on their value, they reign supreme in a land virtually devoid of competition. Until something better comes along to displace them, college rankings, and most notably those by *U.S. News and World Report*, will be what schools advertise.

Although *U.S. News and World Report* is the best-known ranking guide, a trip to the bookstore or a search on the Internet reveals many other ranking guides, all designed to appropriately rank-order institutions based on perceived academic quality or according to other characteristics that editors believe appeal to their core audience. Popular academic rankings include Princeton Review's *The Best 366 Colleges, 2008 Edition*; *The Washington Monthly College Rankings*; and Princeton Review's *College Rankings*. For more holistic rankings, CollegeProwler.com and Wiretap.com both offer what they describe as definitive guides based on information prospective students want to know. Criteria include academic quality, amenities, location, and social life indicators such as fraternity and sorority opportunities and "nightlife."

In addition to the ranking guides, scores of general guides are available from a variety of sources. The most popular include *Peterson's Guide to Four-Year Colleges*, *The College Board's College Handbook*, *Fiske Guide to Colleges*, Princeton Review's *Complete Book of Colleges* and *America's Best Value Colleges*, and *The Insider's Guide to the Colleges*. Because published rankings are somehow considered accurate and unbiased (when compared with information straight from a college or university), readers assume that the college guide books are unbiased reviews as well (Zemsky, Wegner, and Massy, 2005). Ironically, the colleges and universities that are being evaluated by readers of these guidebooks are the same colleges and universities that supply the information and pay extra for extended coverage (Bok, 2003). College guidebooks present an exhaustive list of institutions according to fairly predictable criteria (demographics, location, and academic offerings, for example), but they end up being little more than advertising vehicles for colleges and universities. Schools are able to buy extra space in the guidebooks for a more extensive profile or more detailed information, but readers are left with the impression they are reading unbiased information (Zemsky, Wegner, and Massy, 2005).

College rankings receive far more attention from colleges and universities, the public, and the media, because they are so obviously value laden. The purpose of a rankings list is to do just that: rank. For the public—and often the media that report on the lists—how those rankings were compiled is of less relevance than the actual order itself. Because of their power and their ubiquity, academics have written a great deal about whether or not rankings convey anything meaningful about a college or university (for a good introduction to the topic, see the special section on rankings in the May 25, 2007, issue of *The Chronicle of Higher Education*). Some critics assert that rather than measure "quality," they simply measure "perceptions" of quality (Boyer, 2003; Conard and Conard, 2000). As Boyer (2003) notes, college rankings are riddled with error, often measure insignificant data, and are so arbitrary they are practically meaningless.

Colleges and universities are savvy about promoting the programs that have ranked highly. Frederickson (2001) writes that as *U.S. News and World Report* has modified its rankings over the years to increase the areas of specialization rated, the rankings have been somewhat more favorably received. "In part, this was because finer distinctions allowed more programs to win" (p. 52). For example, a school that did not make the top fifty research universities could claim in promotional materials to rank "number three" in business administration programs because its program was on that list. "Dozens of master's degree programs could now point to their specialized standings and gain at least some bragging rights" (Frederickson, 2001, p. 53).

Although much disagreement exists about the validity of college rankings, almost everyone agrees it is better to be ranked high than it is to be ranked low. Debate on the value of rankings persists, but the fact remains that for many schools, rankings are key to shaping and maintaining brand identity (so long as the ranking is favorable). As I once heard a department chair of a prestigious department at a prestigious university say, "When we're ranking number one, those rankings tell us everything we need to know. When we're not number one? Oh, those rankings are rubbish! Who compiles those silly lists anyway?"

Sarcastic appraisals aside, college ranking lists are big business. Cottage industries have sprung up around the rankings, and a high or low ranking can fundamentally change the way an institution does business.

What is so impressive about the *U.S. News and World Report* rankings is how powerful they are. They are truly the definitive mechanism for positioning colleges and universities. Numerous studies have been conducted and countless opinions abound regarding their fallibility. Regardless of the criticism and the feigned disinterest in wanting to support them or participate in their data collection, most institutions do participate and many do whatever they can to improve their individual ranking.

U.S. News and World Report's rankings dominate market share, reinforce its authority, and strengthen the power it has in the higher education marketing arena. As Brian Kelly, executive editor of *U.S. News* said about rankings, "The reason the rankings are popular is that there is a great hunger among consumers to have some tangible data to use. Some universities are unwilling to give people the information they want . . . . It's not enough to say that this is an unquantifiable, nuanced world, particularly when you are charging people [in some cases] $50,000 a year" (Arnoldy, 2007, p. A6).

College rankings help to establish or propel academic reputation for many colleges and universities. Perceived academic quality plays a significant role in positioning a school (Conard and Conard, 2000), which makes it vitally important as a marketing tool but also complicates advertising efforts, given the difficulty of communicating academic quality in the absence of tangible data.

Conard and Conard's research (2000) reveals that a majority of college-bound high school senior respondents view successful postgraduate careers as very important to the perceptions of academic reputation and that they were more likely to attend a school with a strong academic reputation. Further, "campus ethos" played strongly as a predictive variable for choice.

The implications of this research suggest that colleges and universities should advertise whatever tangible evidence is available that reflects their academic reputation, link that reputation to postgraduate activities (either occupationally or academically), and concentrate efforts to promote the setting and culture of the campus as an ideal location to pursue further study.

Social Life and Campus Amenities

In the search for market differentiation in a world of similarities, colleges and universities heavily advertise an idealized portrait of social life and emphasize campus amenities that often include modern and lavish student housing with gourmet meal plans, state-of-the-art recreation centers, and extraordinary performing arts centers and business schools. Recreation centers alone have undergone massive transformation from the gyms of yesteryear to facilities that feature leisure pools, massage therapy centers, tanning, gravity trainers, spinners, treadmills, stationary bikes, aerobic workout rooms, large flat-screen TVs positioned everywhere, elliptical trainers outfitted with personal TV monitors, racquetball courts, lap pools, rock climbing walls, enormous weight rooms, and coffee shops and cafés (Carlson, 2003; Gose, 2006; McCormack, 2005).

On-campus housing, too, has gone from cramped and dated to spacious and even luxurious. The new generation of students who are "arriving on campuses expects better housing—with an emphasis on more space, more amenities, and more privacy—than previous generations ever would have thought possible" (Kellogg, 2001, p. A37). Luxurious apartment-type residence halls with exotic menus and comfortable common spaces have been erected to meet that need and keep up with similar construction at other institutions. Strategic facility improvements with a focus on customer service training and improved offerings better positions housing as an asset that extends beyond convenience (Parker, Schaefer, Matthews, and Zammuto, 1996, p. 43).

Whether in student unions, recreation centers, or residence halls, "the competition for students is yielding amenities once unimaginable on college campuses, spurring a national debate over the difference between educational necessity and excess" (Winter, 2003, p. A12). Some critics (Capraro, Patrick, and Wilson, 2004; Hayes and Wynyard, 2002; Sperber, 2000) decry the "country clubs" they see colleges and universities morphing into, but Toma, Dubrow, and Hartley (2005) note that institutions have been obsessed with prestige for years and have always used facilities to pursue it. The "contemporary obsession" with the amenities arms race is "entirely consistent with our history of attempting to impress with our campuses" (p. B10). What has changed perhaps is the marketing associated with the construction boom and a more concentrated emphasis on the newly erected facilities.

Rather than capital investment as the new phenomenon, the amenities arms race is likely a reflection of the arms race to market those amenities. Unfortunately, this statement is difficult to assess. A comprehensive literature review in the area of campus amenities and their perceived impact on applications and donations reveals that little research has been done to measure whether a correlation exists between construction and increases in applications, enrollments, and giving. We do know that perceived social life affects student choice and donor behavior (Broekemier and Seshadri, 1999; Kallio, 1995). Campus amenities, like those previously described, create an atmosphere that matches students' expectations about what a campus looks like and the kind of lifestyle one can expect to live. That impression translates into institutional quality assumptions by students, parents, alumni, and donors.

Student choice depends on the impression a campus makes on an applicant, and research indicates that perceived social life is a major factor in student choice (Broekemier and Seshadri, 1999; Kallio, 1995). Capraro, Patrick, and Wilson (2004) found that "attractiveness of social life, defined in terms of characteristics of the people and experiences to be found at a school, is at least as important as quality of education in determining the likelihood of a candidate undertaking decision approach actions toward a school" (p. 93). These actions include requesting information, visiting the campus, or submitting an application. To stimulate these actions, amenities and the social life they host and reflect become vitally important.

Based on these findings, Capraro, Patrick, and Wilson (2004) suggest institutions include marketing content that focuses on personal and social interactions in an attempt to emphasize to prospective students that they will feel comfortable and accepted at the institution. With significance to the amenities available on campus, the authors advise institutions to expand their use of the Web to include "community businesses and facilities that might be of interest to college-aged people" (p. 102). Doing so capitalizes on the school's image "as a place where exciting experiences can be found" (p. 102). The process is made easier when facilities on campus create a community where those things are in close proximity, of high quality, and an extension of the campus itself.

New student recreation centers, student unions, and housing are often difficult to justify to faculty and others, but they are essential components for creating a campus environment prospective students are looking for. As tangible products for marketing, these amenities are highly effective and just part of doing business in the new competitive marketplace. "Enhancing the infrastructure devoted to student life may be a strategic imperative for colleges for the simple reason that competitors are doing it" (Toma, 2006, p. B10). As research has demonstrated (Capraro, Patrick, and Wilson, 2004), perceived social life and the amenities that colleges provide are as important, if not more so, than the academic prestige for many prospective students and their parents. Students need to see tangible evidence that a college or university is a quality institution, and capital improvements provide that information, regardless of whether or not it positively affects one's educational experience. As we have seen all along, perception is often more important than reality.

In addition to the more obvious products of the amenities arms race, some schools have gone to great lengths to achieve market differentiation based on what many would argue are superficial differences at best. The battle over climbing walls demonstrates just how ridiculous the amenities arms race can be. In 2005, the University of Texas at San Antonio unveiled the "tallest climbing wall in Texas" when it erected a fifty-four-foot wall in its newly constructed university recreation center. The height's significance is in the last foot. At fifty-four feet, UTSA's climbing wall was exactly one foot taller than the University of Houston's previous record. Now UTSA has bragging rights for the tallest climbing wall in Texas, which riles Elwyn C. Lee, vice president for student affairs at Houston. "If I could stick a rock on top and glue it down so we would be the tallest, I would" (McCormack, 2005, p. A6).

Mr. Lee would be advised to postpone his rock-gluing efforts, at least temporarily. Texas State University at San Marcos is planning to build what it claims will be the tallest collegiate climbing wall in 2008. The new record? Fifty-five feet, of course.

What this climbing-wall-arms-race-to-the-heavens-over-Texas represents is how desperate many institutions are to have something tangible to communicate quality differences to the community. These peripheral route messages give *something* for administrators to market and promote. Attending a college with the tallest climbing wall in Texas, or anywhere for that matter, is not likely to influence how one learns chemistry. Just being positively talked about among various stakeholder groups in any context, however, allows for peripheral route messaging to occur as well as creates and reinforces affective classical conditioning ("The tallest climbing wall in Texas, you say? Well that's a good thing."). With the tallest climbing wall in Texas, UTSA has something to brag about, and sometimes that is all that matters.

The Halo Effect of a Successful Athletic Program

For many colleges and universities, athletics is the best advertising money can buy—when you are winning, that is. One of the most controversial weapons in the advertising arsenal, a large athletic department can bring attention to a school like no other entity on campus. The conspicuous costs of athletics have raised ire among many members of the university community and the general public, but for advertising and marketing purposes, athletics adds tangibility to an intangible product. The following discussion considers the advantages and disadvantages of allowing so much of one's institutional publicity to rest on the shoulders of the athletic department.

In the public arena of big-time collegiate athletics, critics are calling for all-out reform of a system they see as overrun with commercialism and corruption and, moreover, grossly inconsistent with the academic mission of higher education. Big-time college athletic departments, they say, are moving farther and farther away from the goals and mission of higher education and are simply "feeder-systems" for professional sports. Rather than reflect an institution's academic values, big-time sports do nothing but promote players, coaches, and teams at the university's expense, all the while lining the pockets of advertisers, broadcasters, and others who have a commercial interest in college sports. Critics point out that, although much money can be made in college sports, few colleges or universities have profitable athletic departments. In fact, despite the myth that many successful programs earn millions of dollars for their schools, the reverse is actually true. Except for a tiny minority, most college and university athletic departments run at a deficit that can balloon to millions of dollars per year in red ink.

Defenders of college sports say that colleges and universities have been using their athletic departments to successfully market themselves for years and remind critics that without sports, many Americans would be unable to identify with higher education in any appreciable way. Advocates of big-time programs argue that a successful athletic program is a strong weapon in the university's P.R. arsenal and that the benefits of this exposure justify the expense. Education historian Cohen (1998) writes that "the ostensible mission of the universities—the quest for knowledge and academic excellence—was always subordinate to the institutions' adherence to popular values. They could not stray too far from community mores lest they lose their support" (p. 109). Many supporters argue that big-time college sports merely extends this "adherence to popular values." With the great number of struggling colleges in the University Transformation Era, "each had to promise something to attract students. [The 1840s] was the beginning of the era of brochures and catalogues pointing out the special features of the institution, usually depicted as sitting on the brow of a hill with an expanse of landscape around it, sending the message that one's child would be safe from the evil influences of the city . . . . Each [college] touted the virtues of student life, the associations that students would make, the benefits they would carry with them" (Cohen, 1998, p. 62).

In the modern era, winning teams are that "special feature" of the university and are critical to marketing the university's academics to the general public. In this way, big-time college sports is a kind of "engagement" for many colleges and universities. For many people in a state like Wisconsin, Michigan, Ohio, or North Carolina, the only meaningful contact they might have with their state's universities is through college sports. Presumably, the better the college or university does on the playing field, the greater the connection to the average resident of the state. Does this relationship then build sentiment and support for the college or university in states that depend heavily on a supportive governor and public? If so, it could be argued that big-time college sports programs—even when they operate in the red—are vital to the state's college and university outreach and marketing.

Many colleges and universities are nationally known by their big-time sports programs alone. Is it good for higher education? Should colleges and universities market academics on the shoulders of the athletic department? This question is situated around a Kellogg Commission report (1999) that cites a "seven-part test" that serves as the guiding characteristics in how best to define an "engaged institution" (responsiveness, respect for partners, academic neutrality, accessibility, integration, coordination, and resource partnership). One of the most important roles of engagement is to bring the university and its sense of importance in the community to a broad community level. Supporters of college sports argue that sports make it possible by bringing the residents of the community something about the university to get excited about—a winning sports program.

The Kellogg report states that "the university is a near-inscrutable entity governed by its own mysterious sense of itself. It's difficult to get a grip on this institution, understand its points of leverage, and find a way through the academic maze" (p. 20). Sports cut through this confusion to give a unified and collective picture of the university. To do so, student-athletes are emphasized, the culture and climate of the school are shown through fan participation, and advertising showcases the "whole" university during games. This kind of advertising regularly appears during sports broadcasting at all levels as advertisements are broadcast by individual colleges, conferences, and the National Collegiate Athletic Association itself. What this situation creates is a cultural icon of higher education as the preeminent destination for those set on achieving excellence on or off the field.

Although probably not what the Kellogg Commission had in mind when it researched and wrote the report, I call this "entertainment engagement." It is the most universal and easily recognized way that colleges and universities "engage" with the broader public, and it is a powerful mechanism for engagement. Many schools market themselves through the strength of their athletic department. Whether it is in appeals to alumni for donations or in recruitment literature sent to prospective students, sports is everywhere, and few schools are willing to shy away from a winning season. The Kellogg report (1999) indicates that for successful engagement, resource partnerships must be established. "The most successful engagement efforts appear to be those associated with strong and healthy relationships with partners in government, business, and the non-profit world" (p. 12). Big-time college sports is an offshoot of that engagement spirit and helps forge key relationships with many resource partners. In fact, many relationships with politicians and business leaders are created and maintained at sporting events (for a detailed profile of this kind of relationship-building, see Selingo, 2001).

In many ways, the "advertising" that many colleges and universities receive from their big-time athletic programs supports engagement efforts in the community and contributes to a culture of success. Unlike the biology or philosophy departments, the community really can "rally around the team." Whether or not this "rallying" is meaningful is not the point. Rather, it is something about which the average citizen can get excited when it comes to a college or university, and in that respect the "advertising" could pay off in unforeseen ways.

A visible athletic program does three things well: (1) it creates something tangible for people to rally around; (2) it enables brand communities to flourish by providing something for which the brand has relevance and more closely binds people to the brand and the community; and (3) it provides advertisement through televised games, both regional and national.

Because big-time college sports is not part of the "academic mission" of higher education per se, it is largely considered a transient, trivial topic. This attitude is a mistake. Most members of the larger community (the public) make an association with their local college or university only because of its sports programs. For this reason, college and university personnel must better understand the role of big-time sports programs as they relate to the academic mission and the university as a whole. True for matters of governance, it is especially true for the marketing and advertising that occurs as a result of a visible athletic department.

The visibility athletics provides is valuable in its scope and reach and difficult to replicate in any other way for colleges and universities. After all, how else can an average-sized school, with average-sized accomplishments and no meaningful national presence, assert itself into Americans' daily lives? The reason big-time college sports programs have opened the door for brand identity for some colleges and universities is because of opportunities for mere exposure ("Did you see the Notre Dame–USC game last night?") and affective conditioning ("You should have seen Reggie Bush's touchdowns. They featured him on SportsCenter last night. It was incredible.") they create. In both the examples just cited, USC is talked about, while the University of San Francisco is not. For schools looking to recruit students regionally and nationally, this kind of sustained marketing has profound effect on building name recognition.

Regardless of whether or not a team wins, just being on television allows a school to communicate who they are and allows them to be included in the group of schools on television. Winning is not as important as just being seen, which provides a subtle cultivation opportunity for branding. People, especially potential students, are not likely to remember how many games a particular team wins or loses, but the mere exposure and coverage of the school communicates to the applicant that it has quality. Perceived institutional quality increases with television exposure.

When prospective students who are not athletes use an institution's athletic department as part of the school selection process, they are being strongly influenced by peripheral route messaging that is intended to reflect perceived institutional quality. If a prospective student stopped and thoughtfully considered how a successful college athletic program would affect her education or learning in higher education, she might realize that no relationship exists between the two. In fact, she might even conclude that a negative relationship exists. A Rose Bowl victory does not a good college education make. But it is doubtful that the average prospective student is that reflective and examines those relationships; she might rather be dazzled by marketing and advertising that makes a winning program a tangible feature of a college or university and its perceived quality.

The question, of course, is whether or not marketing and advertising on the shoulders of a successful and visible athletic department is sound judgment for university administrators. Fortunately, research in the area of successful athletics and applications gives us some sense of the advertising and marketing efficacy of college sports programs.

The Cost of "Advertising" and the "Flutie Factor." The play that will be forever remembered took place November 23, 1984, at the Orange Bowl in Miami, Florida. With one Hail Mary pass into the end zone on a last-second play, quarterback Doug Flutie led his Boston College team to victory over the Miami Hurricanes 45–41. A media frenzy followed—and so did the applications to attend Boston College. The year after Flutie's miracle pass was completed, applications jumped 25 percent at the small Boston college, and the term "Flutie Factor" was born.

Simply put, the Flutie Factor suggests that national success and attention in big-time college sports drives prospective students to apply. It is a phrase and an idea repeated so often that it is almost accepted as gospel in higher education: big wins bring students. A certain logic surrounds the Flutie Factor, and few question the truth behind the legend.

But just how much truth is there to the Flutie Factor? Skeptics and believers abound. Phillip Ballinger, Gonzaga University's dean of admissions, made the leap from skeptic to believer after Gonzaga's pool of applicants swelled by 72 percent in the three years following their unprecedented success in men's basketball in the 1990s. After three NCAA tournament appearances, Gonzaga was transformed from an unknown private school in the state of Washington to a bona fide contender. "I still couldn't accept that something like [a winning team] would matter when it comes to such an important decision, but I've become a believer" (Greenwald, 2001, p. A7).

Research seeking to measure big-time college sports success and its potential impact on college applications finds generally positive relationships. Toma and Cross (1998) conducted a longitudinal study of national championship winners and the impact winning has on the number of undergraduate applications a school receives. They found that "notable increases generally occurred in admissions applications received—both in absolute terms but more importantly relative to peer schools—in the years following the championship season" (p. 633). Similarly, Chu (1989) found a positive correlation between athletic success and freshman applicants over a ten-year period in a study of the large Division I conferences (Pac-10, Big Ten, Big East, ACC, SEC, WAC, and Ivy League), as did Chressanthis and Grimes (1993) in a related study.

Most relevant to this monograph is the conclusion that McCormick and Tinsley (1990) draw when they write that collegiate athletics makes an important contribution to higher education through "advertisement." "College athletic contests attract viewers and media attention, which lure prospective students, faculty, and donors, and maintain contact between alumni and alma mater" (p. 193). In addition, increased attention drives up the number of applications, enabling colleges to pick the best students from a larger pool. They conclude that as the number of applicants rise, so too does the quality of students as measured by SAT scores.

It is important to note that in many of the studies seeking to measure the relationship between athletic success and undergraduate applications, the authors conclude that athletic success is but one factor among many that influences where a student decides to attend college. Other factors include the perceived quality of education the school offers, the school's overall reputation, and the direct cost of education to students (see McCormick and Tinsley, 1990; Rhoads and Gerking, 2000; Sack and Watkins, 1985; and Sigelman and Carter, 1979, among others).

This finding suggests that having a winning and visible big-time college athletic program contributes to a cultural atmosphere of success on the field, in the classroom, and across campus. Success on Saturday afternoons is but one facet of a multisuccessful institution and can help contribute to a culture of "perceived success" when seen in aggregate form.

In addition to this kind of cultural impact, key players in college sports recruiting see real effects when their teams win. Many claim that a winning season brings in more diverse applicants. "That rings true for Robert M. Bontrager, director of admissions at Oregon State University, who has seen a 35 percent bump over last year in the number of out-of-state applications received since the Beavers beat the University of Notre Dame 41–9 in the Fiesta Bowl on January 1 [2001]" (Suggs, 2001, p. A51). Despite this increase, Bontrager acknowledges that he "would far prefer they find us because they find our academic programs compelling, and our student-life programs will help them have the kind of career they want to have . . . but the reality is that for some students, we gain an opportunity because of playing Notre Dame on New Year's Day and winning" (Suggs, 2001, p. A51).

Bontrager also says that even though students do not say they choose a university because its teams appear on national television, sometimes they do subconsciously. "If you ask someone who chose a particular product or service, in many cases they will cite reasons other than advertising . . . . If you ask them, 'We had a billboard in your area—did that influence your decision?' they often will say, 'Oh, no. I have much more significant, substantial, qualitative reasons why I made that choice,' when in reality, when you look at buying patterns, you find significant bumps where there is mass-market advertising. That's in effect when we talk about things like our Fiesta Bowl win" (Suggs, 2001, p. A51).

The ultimate question is whether or not colleges and universities receive enough through donations and advertising (in its various forms) to justify the enormous expense and the unrelenting criticism that big-time college sports programs contribute little to the academic mission of a college or university. And how much of a role does television exposure play in this debate? Does a regular presence on national television affect a college or university in measurable ways and, if so, where? Television allows a school to have a broad reach, far beyond what was otherwise imaginable. Does it make a difference?

A Difference of Opinion: Intercollegiate Athletics and Big-Time College Sports. If the old adage "everyone has an opinion" were ever true, it is in the arena of big-time college sports. To really understand the complexities of this topic, it is important to know that everyone involved has an opinion and much of that opinion is based on anecdotal evidence and inconclusive research. One must also know that the current literature is dominated by critics of big-time college sports and that few are writing or publishing a response that defends the other side. The literature in defense of athletics that does exist generally contains reports of inconclusive research and other writing by critics and supporters who admit some good things come out of big-time college sports (for example, the advertising effect, building a stronger campus community, and so on).

The past twenty-five years have seen a surge in the number of books calling for reform in big-time college sports programs. At the forefront of the criticism is Murray Sperber, professor emeritus, Indiana University. Sperber has written a number of books on college sports, including *College Sports, Inc.: The Athletic Department vs. the University* (1990), in which he introduces the idea of college sports as big business; *Onward to Victory: The Crises That Shaped College Sports* (1998), which traces many of the abuses of intercollegiate athletics; and *Beer and Circus: How Big-Time College Sports Is Crippling Undergraduate Education* (2000). Sperber's books are joined by others (Andre and James, 1991; Duderstadt, 2000; Lawrence, 1987; Sack and Staurowsky, 1998; Shulman and Bowen, 2001; Telander, 1996; Zimbalist, 1999) calling for a reexamination of the role intercollegiate athletics plays on campus, especially with regard to football and men's basketball, which critics say have become nothing but overcommercialized, semiprofessional teams.

It is *Beer and Circus* (2000) that has drawn the most fire from supporters of college athletics, as Sperber claims that universities, especially the largest Division I schools, have given up on the idea of delivering a quality education to their undergraduates and are instead creating campuses that serve to entertain students. This "beer and circus" environment that encourages students to rally around the team as "entertainment" becomes the core product of their higher education experience, not a quality education. He maintains that this atmosphere keeps students distracted from questioning the value of their education and instead urges them to "party around the team" on a campus that is constantly "on spring break" (2000, p. 19). Sperber argues that this "distraction" frees up faculty to work with graduate students and on their research (a major source of funding for schools) and frees up the administration from working to improve life in the classroom for undergraduate students. Having a high-profile, big-time college sports program provides the necessary distraction and entertainment for students to feel they are having a "genuine college experience" without the administrative burden of providing a high-quality education.

Sperber (2000) also maintains that the problem is escalating based on the television broadcasting factor. "The main difference between the early 1980s and now is summed up in four letters—ESPN," which allows fans to spend "every waking hour within SportsWorld. Never before in history was this possible" (p. 40). Sperber documents how ESPN plays a role in feeding fans' obsession with college sports and the creation of new, ravenous fans. He also discusses how ESPN's programming has changed scheduling for NCAA basketball games (and now football) and has transformed the average game into a "must-see" event through daily shows like SportsCenter (p. 43).

In many ways, televising more college sports encouraged interest from the broader public and reversed a decline from thirty years ago. "In the 1970s and 1980s, the lack of interest in college sports not only separated academics from the mainstream of university life at many schools, but also from an important component of popular culture outside the university" (p. 21). As the electronic media "ratcheted up the coverage of all sports, especially intercollegiate athletics, more students embraced their college teams than previously, and more members of the general public became sports fans" (p. 21). Television created increased interest and helped make college sports ubiquitous not only in the public's mind but also in the minds of college and university advertisers.

In addition, Sperber believes the biggest impact that television has had on viewers is what he says is the "equivalent of what George Orwell defined in *1984* as 'doublethink': the ability to believe contradictory ideas simultaneously, for example, acknowledging the dysfunction of college sports while fervently following its teams and games" (p. 42). This attitude sits squarely on the shoulders of many followers of college sports: the ability to follow and support college sports, all the while recognizing its myriad abuses. This doublethink also leaks into the minds of marketing units on college and university campuses. Although they know a Final Four appearance in the NCAA men's basketball tournament will not affect learning or academics, marketing folks are quick to point out how success on the floor merely reflects the excellence that extends across all units on campus.

Finally, Sperber as well as others (Duderstadt, 2000; Zimbalist, 1999) believe that college athletes are nothing more than unpaid professionals and that the amateurism of college sports is a fraud; the atmosphere swirling around college sports has become too commercial and too professional to really believe it benefits the larger campus community beyond satisfying individual interests (Sperber, 1998, 2000). Of those interests is the marketing and advertising benefit institutions receive as a result of their sports programs.

Like Sperber, James Duderstadt (2000), former president of the University of Michigan at Ann Arbor, believes big-time college sports differ little from their professional counterparts. For him, a team's focus on "commercial value" and "market share" are often the main goal in developing and maintaining the team's success. Both improve the team's visibility in the competitive marketplace and ostensibly improve the athletic image and visibility of the school they represent. The welfare of players as students, he asserts, is largely ignored. Instead, Duderstadt maintains that conferences (like the Big 10) operate more like professional leagues, except that they do not have to pay income tax on what they earn. Zimbalist (1999) agrees with Duderstadt's financial analysis of big-time college sports and provides strong economic evidence to support his idea that college students are simply professionals masquerading as amateurs.

By its very nature, Duderstadt (2000) complains, "Big-time college athletics has little to do with the nature or objectives of the contemporary university. Instead, it is a commercial venture, aimed primarily at public entertainment for those beyond the campus and at generating rewards for those who stage it" (p. 11). The public, he argues, is "driven by the sports media and commercial interests, seeks from our universities entertainment through football and basketball, staged at a commercial level in every way comparable to professional leagues" (p. 11).

The big question for Duderstadt is "whether or not this particular form of public entertainment should be the responsibility of the university?" (p. 12). He acknowledges that the contemporary university "engages in many forms of public service" and cites examples such as health care through university medical centers and technology that reaches the marketplace through relationships with private enterprise (p. 12). The difference, he says, is that each of these activities "has firm roots within the academic mission of the university" and involves faculty and students "who participate as a 'component' of their educational mission" (p. 12).

Shulman and Bowen (2001), in one of the most comprehensive studies done on college sports, present results of what they say is groundbreaking research examining the current state of intercollegiate athletics. Their study focused on ninety thousand undergraduate students—athletes and others—who entered a total of thirty colleges and universities at three time: the fall semesters of 1951, 1976, and 1989. What they found is that the gap between sports and education has been broadening over time at Division I institutions as well as at Ivy League and selective liberal arts colleges. Their research results suggest that what Sperber (2000) describes could be a reality.

Shulman and Bowen's research (2001) suggests that, instead of improving practice at these schools, more admissions, recruiting, and academic abuses are likely to occur, which can lead to faculty alienation and dissatisfaction. Without college leadership intervention, "the growing gap between college athletics and education values" is inevitable and will "continue to be a major, unavoidable, issue for the academy" (p. 294). Further, they write that the gap must be understood and addressed: "The objective should be to reinvigorate the contribution of intercollegiate athletics to the achievement of educational goals" (p. 294). Ultimately, "the goal would be to identify collective solutions that respect local circumstances and institutional priorities. In the absence of effective action, the underlying conflicts between college sports and educational values will only get worse" (p. 294).

In an argument similar to Duderstadt's (2000), Sack (2001) observes that big-time college sports is all about entertainment and that people must like it the way it is, or there would be more efforts to change the system. Like many writers on the subject, Sack personally likes the idea "of spinning off big-time football and basketball programs as independent professional franchises" (2001, p. B7). This sentiment echoes across campuses as college sports coverage expands to even the smallest television markets.

Although not much has been written to refute the charges of many of today's big-time sports critics, some writers support big-time college sports and the role it plays on campus. Anecdotally, supporters of big-time athletics (men's basketball and football) point out that a strong athletic department functions as a kind of "engagement" agent in the community, helps to build alumni support, is a tool for marketing a school's academics, provides access to important lobbyists, and often funds the entire athletic department.

Supporters argue that many athletic departments that operate at a deficit do so because of the expense of non-revenue-producing sports and many women's programs. In fact, these same big-time programs would actually make a profit if they functioned on their own and did not have to fill holes in the department budget (Farrell, 1989). Farrell reminds readers that, "without the support of basketball and football, many institutions would be hard pressed to offer women's sports, which have expanded and gained acceptance in their rightful place alongside men's" (p. 15).

In addition, successful programs can have a positive effect on a school's culture. As Duderstadt (2000) notes, "College sports permeate . . . university communities as their culture revolves around these events [sports], season by season: football in the fall, basketball and hockey in the winter, the NCAA tournaments in the spring. Merchants, restaurants, and hotels depend on football crowds" (p. 3). Moreover, alumni are "bound to their institutions by the common experience of returning each year for a football weekend or attending a bowl game or an NCAA tournament" (p. 3). Duderstadt goes on to say that "big-time intercollegiate athletics, when kept in balance with academic life, can contribute in a positive way to a college education. Varsity sports can provide unifying events that pull together the . . . complex and diverse communities that make up the contemporary university" (p. 10).

In response to a study that calls into question the impact of a winning team on recruitment, John Maguire, former dean of admissions for Boston College, says that his consulting company's research on influences of big-time college sports reveals that "multivariate modeling often unearths hidden variables as predictors," one of which is athletics. In addition, he says that "when we analyze prestige, we find it is frequently correlated with big-time athletics," which students report have a positive effect on "the quality of student life and on retention" (Maguire, 2001, p. B18).

History professor David McDonald, academic liaison with the University of Wisconsin–Madison athletic department, is quick to point out that the "moralization" by critics on the issue bears deeper analysis. McDonald says that the rest of the university should be held to the same standards as the athletic department with regard to outside relations with private industry. If it were, it too would be subject to criticism regarding deals with many private businesses that profit from the university. McDonald says that part of the problem with "mission" in this debate is that the university's mission is so ill defined campuswide (personal communication, 2001).

The existing empirical research in the area of big-time college sports and their impact on colleges and universities is inconclusive at best. Past studies have focused most of their attention on university enrollment trends and voluntary support of education (donations) to measure the role that success (or failure) plays in motivating alumni to give to their alma mater and motivating new students to enroll. In general, different study methods employed over the years have unearthed diverse findings that have led to contradictory conclusions on all sides of the debate.

What have come from much of the research on the effects of visible sports programs are theories to explain why sports remain so popular as a mechanism for marketing and advertising (despite the difficulty of measuring said results). Gaski and Etzel (1984) suggest that "there may be a more complex relationship between collegiate athletics and benefactor donations than would be revealed by the type of analysis reported in the literature so far," including their own study. They speculate that "perhaps successful football and basketball teams do have an impact on fund-raising but only as a cumulative effect built up over a great number of years" (p. 31). In this case, success on the field "enhances a school's public image [that], ultimately, translates into increased donations" (p. 31). Gaski and Etzel's conclusion suggests that exposure through various media, just for the sake of exposure, could have a direct effect on a college or university in predicted ways. Perhaps the mere exposure of a college or university to a wider audience, not the relative success or failure of the sports team, becomes the predictor.

Despite not finding a strong link between winning and alumni giving at select schools, Sack and Watkins (1985) also suggest that just having a football team may be enough for many alumni. "College sport is often at the center of campus social life. Around it has grown homecoming, football weekends, and a wide variety of collegiate rituals [that] keep alumni in touch with their schools" (p. 304). This observation has implications for brand community development and could translate to great action based on indirect advertising appeal and exposure.

Based on their research, Rhoads and Gerking (2000) propose that the payoff for building a successful athletic program may come more quickly than building strong academic programs because donors are able to judge the improvements more readily. It is much easier to witness success on the field, especially if "prospective donors have difficulty judging academic improvements and changes in academic reputation lag behind actual improvements" (p. 257). Athletics, then, becomes a tangible feature for alumni (and others) to attach themselves to.

Baade and Sundberg (1996) caution that although "colleges and universities seem to be rewarded by their alumni for sports programs that are extremely successful . . . investment in athletic programs carries with it risks" (p. 802). Additional spending on athletics "does not necessarily result in more successful teams or more postseason appearances" (p. 802). Many variables account for a winning or losing season beyond just the number of dollars spent on the athletic department or an individual team. Thinking one can "buy" success through financial support for an athletic department is a dangerous trap that may yield few results for the investor.

Similarly, McCormick and Tinsley (1990) conclude that collegiate athletics makes an important contribution to higher education through what they call "advertisement." Their study of 150 Division I colleges and universities examined the impact of successful football programs on the number of undergraduate applications an institution received and found that application numbers increase with success and lead to a higher-quality freshman class. "College athletic contests attract viewers and media attention, which lure prospective students, faculty, and donors, and maintain contact between alumni and alma mater" (p. 193). In addition, increased attention drives up the number of applications, enabling colleges to pick the best students from a larger pool. They concluded that as the number of applicants rises, so too does the quality of students, as measured by SAT scores (p. 179). Their research refutes the popular belief that donations to the athletic department represent lost revenue to the academic endowment. According to their study, "There is no evidence that athletic booster club fundraising crowds out philanthropic donations to the academic endowment" (p. 200).

The most convincing evidence linking winning and giving comes from a handful of scenarios in which a school experiences a dramatic shift in its win-loss record. Sigelman and Carter (1979) cite examples like Ohio State in 1966, the University of Missouri in 1960, and the University of Georgia in 1961. In all these cases, alumni support seems to rise impressively with the team's sudden good fortune.

It is important to note that in many of the studies that measure the effect of success on the field and an increase in applications, the authors conclude that athletic success is but one factor among many that influence where a student decides to attend college. Other factors include the perceived quality of education, the reputation of the institution, and cost.

If athletic success is "but one quality among many" that drives student choice, it could affect how an institution is perceived individually and relative to its peers. "Most admissions officers, even most presidents and provosts, intuitively understand that students think not so much of individual institutions as of groups of institutions. In the words of one veteran dean of admissions, 'We are known primarily by the company we keep'" (Zemsky and Oedel, 1983, p. 45).

Colleges and universities that wish for a national presence might be well served by seeking to elevate their status by expanding or enriching the company they keep. One way to do so is by focusing attention on a successful athletic program, especially one that is in the spotlight. "For reasons that are not entirely clear . . . prominence in sports is equated in the public mind with the academic reputation and prestige—or at least it is in the opinion of public relations experts on higher education" (Hanford, 1974, p. 54). National success, in any form, is rarely frowned on in higher education, and why would it be? "Success in sports is seen as helpful in getting the name of the institution before the public, in attracting students, in hiring faculty, and raising money. Certainly most institutions that have tried to upgrade themselves academically in recent years, most of them large and most of them public, have accompanied the effort with new emphases on their sports programs" (Hanford, 1974, p. 54). Institutional excellence, by whatever means, remains institutional excellence.

Despite these ambitions, warnings from all sides abound. Although football and men's basketball may have some positive benefits for some institutions (increased visibility and increased revenue, among others), big-time college sports comes packaged with drawbacks. As Spaeth and Greeley (1970) caution with regard to building winning football programs, "One need only point out that the production of such a phenomenon is transient, expensive, chancy, and potentially in conflict with other goals to realize that this is hardly the basis for a viable fiscal policy" (p. 211).

This whole debate begs the question of whether colleges and universities should be in the business of providing public entertainment through intercollegiate sports. "There turns out to be a wide difference of opinion, the implications of which should be the subject of careful scrutiny in a national study" (Hanford, 1974, p. 65). More than thirty years later, the question persists and agreement on all sides seems far off. Regardless, "there is no doubt that big-time college sports programs are in fact in the entertainment business whether they like it or not" (p. 65). And part of being in the entertainment business is succeeding. Television's largest share of revenue goes to the teams that do well and draw big crowds. The teams most often on television are there because they succeed most often. This fact puts tremendous pressure on coaches and players to produce winning teams. A history of criticism is built on evidence suggesting that big-time college sports, in its commercial entertainment form, undermines many academic values (Hanford, 1974; Savage et al., 1929; Underwood, 1980); critics warn that increased television only further undermines those values as more teams vie for coverage. One thing is certain, for the short term at least, big-time college sports on television is here to stay.

Promotional Materials and Communication

Promotional materials have been a significant component of the college and university marketing machine for decades. Viewbooks, the Internet, and other communication tools (such as e-mail and Internet messaging) are pure niche marketing that seeks to appeal to a very specific and narrowly defined audience. Niche marketing depends on understanding the target market's needs and creating information and advertising that will appeal to and encourage action on the part of that market audience.

Results from a survey of university students and the impact promotional materials had on their college choice (Armstrong and Lumsden, 1999) found that materials and information need to be up to date and accurate above everything else. The institution must ensure that the materials it produces and distributes are accurate and complete but also that they genuinely reflect the full range of intellectual and social offerings the campus has to offer. Whatever the information is, and whatever format it takes, honesty (within reason) is the best policy regarding information creation and dissemination (Tinto, 1987).

Promotional materials should contain all the information a reasonable prospective student expects to find. Information about academic offerings, housing, dining, services, and financial aid should all be easy to navigate and understand. Although the lesson applies to other areas as well, Hossler, Schmit, and Vesper (1999) write that "the information on financial aid and college costs should be simple. . . . Parents and students simply need to know that financial aid is available to help. . . . Parents should be constantly reminded that the tuition at most colleges . . . is not $30,000 a year" (p. 29). Promotional materials and other information provide an opportunity for schools to address common myths about higher education in general and specifically for their institution.

Beyond just the content, Armstrong and Lumsden (1999) discovered that to be effective, colleges and universities should "include more photographs and employ bright colors and more unique shapes" in what they produce. In addition to visual layout, materials need to "speak the students' language and show campus life in realistic, relevant ways." Students are looking for a good "fit" and a place "where 'a person like me will feel comfortable'" (Karp, Holmstrom, and Gray, 1998, p. 275). A clearly communicated message that reflects the realities of campus and campus life is the best strategy for relaying institutional identity.

Armstrong and Lumsden (1999) conclude that although a college or university is a traditional place, "marketing its strengths and benefits to today's students may require non-traditional methods" (p. 90)—especially with the shifting nature of student language, communication platforms, and information retrieval. The Internet, social networking, and new forms of digital engagement are revolutionizing how colleges and universities communicate with their niche audiences, making adherence to the core characteristics of good promotional communication more vital than ever so they do not get lost in the message itself.

Viewbooks

Despite the shift toward information's being largely provided electronically (through the Internet), traditional printed viewbooks still play a major role in college and university promotions. Although an institutional Web site generally offers all the same information as a printed viewbook (and often far more and with greater detail), colleges and universities continue to send viewbooks in large volume to target audiences, and they remain a staple in the promotional toolbox (Furbeck, 2003).

As colleges and universities consider the content of their viewbooks, they need to ask themselves who they are, what their core mission is, and whether the viewbook reflects that core mission. Do we "look" different from our competition, and have we articulated what makes us different in a tangible way that considers our market audience's perceived needs and expectations?

In a study that sought to measure content group differences between top-ranked and lower-ranked college and university viewbooks, Klassen (2000) found that clear categorical differences exist between the two groups regarding the content of their viewbooks. For example, top-ranked schools had significantly higher proportions of images showing students engaged in artistic activities, students attending class, technology, and faculty, either in greater numbers or in detailed profiles. By contrast, lower-ranked schools had a significantly higher proportion of images showing outdoor beauty; students involved in intramural sports and viewing varsity sports; fairs, carnivals, and parades; and student and alumni profiles.

Klassen (2000) concludes that the group differences reflect a completely different message to the niche audience about the kind of experience that awaits them at the various campuses. For the top-ranked schools, the message reflects the audience group's expectation that the college or university will help them develop research skills, allow them access to faculty through personal contact, and create an environment that supports their academic aspirations. Conversely, the lower-ranked schools communicate an image that "implies a passive relationship between organization and consumer [that] is commonly seen in commercials for consumer products, such as beer and laundry detergent, which show people deriving personal benefits from the product usage" (p. 17).

These findings are critical in that they reflect how higher education operates along a line of assumptions regarding what students (and their parents) expect to see in an institution. Knowing who you are and who you are trying to reach is important for meeting or altering those expectations. Klassen writes that for both groups (and for colleges and universities in general), the viewbook has come to play a central role in how colleges and universities are marketed. More than just a "collection of flattering" pictures, however, viewbooks have come to be institutional symbols of values and priorities; they "match product and organizational image with the needs of particular students thereby communicating who will and will not feel comfortable attending the schools they represent" (p. 20). The images and differences between groups examined in the study reflect the different niche audience needs of higher and lower academic demands, as they also reflect how different institutional types are likely to advertise and promote themselves in established market niches.

Unfortunately, Klassen's most disturbing finding (2000) is not examined in as much detail as group differences. Klassen writes that "for fully half of the viewbooks examined [in this study], the perspective of college life offered is practically devoid of commitment and loyalty to anything beyond having a good time while waiting to graduate" (p. 21). If this observation can be generalized to college and university marketing across institutions nationally (and given the top-ranked and lower-ranked schools in the population sample, it would appear that generalizability is possible), then the message is clear: colleges and universities might be advertising the permanent vacation critics fear is beginning to define higher education marketing and reality (Hayes and Wynyard, 2002; Sperber, 2000; Thacker, 2005). It is not within the scope of this monograph to take up that issue, but recognizing that viewbooks market lifestyle above almost everything else does reflect the changing market expectations for the kind of experience prospective college students expect to see and eventually have.

In the past fifteen years, viewbooks have begun to take an alternative form. Digital products meant to communicate the "virtual campus" are being produced and distributed to prospective students and donors all over the country.

Like their printed cousins of yesteryear, a whole new kind of viewbook is emerging from college and university marketing departments. Virtual tour DVDs, CD-ROMs, and even video games are becoming common tools in recruiting prospective students (Doherty, 2002; Furbeck, 2003; Hite and Yearwood, 2001). As we will see shortly in the discussion of institutional Web sites, digital products offer greater flexibility for distribution, great range for information dissemination, and the ability to continually edit and revise. A viewbook that can take multiple forms greatly expands the advertising and promotional reach of the marketing department and should be considered after a cost-benefit analysis has been conducted.

Web Sites and the Internet

A visually attractive and easy to use Web site is often the first impression a college or university makes. Even before requesting information or expressing interest, prospective students and others will visit an institution's Web site and search for information, tour various areas, and make critical decisions. Judy Hingle, director of professional development at the National Association for College Admission Counseling, says the Internet has changed from being a supplement to materials that colleges and universities use to recruit to being the first source. "For a great majority of students, [a school's Web site] is going to be their first impression. This is going to be their handshake" (Carnevale, 2005, p. A25).

Because the college Web site has become such a critical communication tool, it is essential that institutions create an online "virtual self" that is aesthetically pleasing, easy to use, informative, and accurate (Cox and Dale, 2002; Foster, 2003; Kittle, 2001; Stoner, 2004; Tedeschi, 2004). Information that is available online allows a college or university to articulate those things that cannot be communicated because of its inherent limitations (such as its relatively small size and the inability to alter information once it is printed). Online information dissemination allows for an articulated message to be constantly changing and accurate. Out-of-date information can be updated relatively effortlessly, and more dramatic content change is possible without the expense and effort of reprinting materials and redistributing them.

The first encounter with an institutional Web page is critical for successful marketing to potential students. These potential students spend hours online every week, and they have an intuitive sense about how a Web page should be laid out and the ease with which it should be navigated. This population has no problem ordering clothes online, purchasing and downloading music and videos, and doing much of their communicating through a digital medium. Their expectations for the kind of information a Web site offers have been calibrated by commercial heavy hitters like Amazon.com, Nike, Apple, and MTV. It is easy to appear amateur in a world featuring that kind of technological firepower, and every effort needs to be made to avoid common mistakes that lead to poorly designed Web pages.

As an advertising tool, the online gateway to the college or university is critical in creating a positive and lasting first impression. Just as important is avoiding a negative experience online. Students reason, rightfully so, that if the online site is difficult to navigate, what is the rest of campus like? If I were on campus, would it be this hard for me to find where my classes are? How can I access financial aid? How can I learn about parking? Where can I eat, and what is there to do?

The Web site for any institution should send the same message and create the same "face" to the institution as print materials currently do (Adelman, 2006; Cox and Dale, 2002). Clifford Adelman, a senior associate at the Institute for Higher Education Policy, has strong recommendations for colleges and universities when it comes to content of the Web page. Adelman believes that labels for "prospective students," "future students," and "new students" must be located in "prime visual real estate" (2006, p. B26). He advises against embedding these buttons in the "admissions" label, as some high school students might not intuitively think to go there. Further, he recommends that all college and university Web pages have a "contact us" button as well as a "search" box.

Besides following the general architecture and design of standard Web sites, Adelman (2006) believes high school students have special interests when considering a college or university, and those interests should be considered when designing online content that will appeal to them. Applications procedures and deadlines are critically important to this population. Likewise, information about tuition and fees and about financial aid and paying for college should be clearly accessible. Definitions and procedures regarding the financial aspects of attendance are important but often neglected. Advisement and orientation should be part of a section on registration that also includes what students can expect in the first year. Finally, college and university personnel must see their campus's Web page through the eyes of prospective students. "Adopt a student persona" and take a tour of the Web site, Adelman advises. Create a list of things you want to know about an institution and then see whether you can navigate your institution's Web page and find the information without much difficulty. Is information presented logically? Is it possible to always find your way back to a root menu or the home page? Does the Web site have the information you seek in places you, as a prospective student, expect to find it?

If not, redesign is an important consideration. Redesigning a Web site can be costly and time consuming, but the payoff can be worth the effort. To stay competitive in a constantly evolving technological world, one must be responsive and provide accurate information in an easy-to-navigate package. A customer is unlikely to purchase something he or she does not feel comfortable using or that lacks complete information. For colleges and universities, that decision might be made at the first digital handshake.

In their research on college and university Web site content, Ramasubramanian, Gyure, and Mursi (2002) found that visuals on the Web site can convey a powerful message about an institution and its mission. Their findings strongly suggest that "college-bound students do form impressions about the more abstract qualities of an institution on the basis of visual images of its physical identity" (p. 64). Students in their study formed strong impressions of academic quality in response to "traditional architectural representations" on Web pages. The findings suggest that during the early stages of a college search, students associate "quality with what they think they know, rather than with the unusual or unfamiliar" (p. 64). In other words, traditional buildings and architecture represented on a Web site or in viewbooks confirm expectations of a quality institution. The authors suggest that strong visual images grounded in traditional architecture convey a sense of institutional longevity, history, and traditions. If the college or university looks good, it must be good.

In addition to these findings, Ramasubramanian, Gyure, and Mursi (2002) report that the presence of landscaping imagery (such as trees, expansive grounds, and rolling lawns) contributes to the same impressions of academic reputation as architecture. They conclude that "academic prestige is, in a sense, landscaped, orderly" (p. 65). What is most interesting is how this assumption about prestige is then transferred to impressions of athletic reputation as well. The authors speculate that the presence of "greenery" translates into positive impressions of athletics as well as aesthetics, which has implications for the halo effect of positive assumptions discussed in "The Halo Effect of a Successful Athletic Program." It also indicates that an easy-to-navigate self-guided virtual tour is a basic necessity for prospective students, who visit a Web site with a set of expectations that are largely abstract and based on perception. Institutions must provide a context to bring these abstractions into focus on something concrete.

A campus presentation that is well landscaped and includes architecturally pleasing images is most likely to deliver content that prospective students expect to see. Fulfilling this expectation will help form positive impressions of greater academic reputation, a strong athletic program, and overall elevated prestige. Perhaps a student visits a Web site with strong preconceived notions of characteristics a "good" institution will have. It should look like a good college (with historic elements and facilities), it should be set where a good college is set (in a largely bucolic setting that is aesthetically pleasing), and it should contain elements of spectator sports that one associates with a college or university.

Ramasubramanian, Gyure, and Mursi's research (2002) supports this three-part set of assumptions, which becomes instructive for Web site design and content. Their findings have significant implications for advertising and marketing the elements and characteristics of a campus. Students go to Web sites and page through viewbooks looking for clues to the academic reputation of a college or university. They have preconceived ideas about what elements should be present to communicate strong academic reputation and quality education. Ensuring those clues are obvious leads to better impressions and will likely translate to action on the part of prospective students and other constituents.

Finally, a successful Web presence depends on how easy it is for students to find you in the first place. Colleges and universities should actively monitor how they come up in queries on search engines like Google and Yahoo. The goal is to appear at the top of as many search queries involving colleges or universities as possible. By tweaking an institution's Web site and megatags (the hidden descriptive language about Web pages that search engines use to generate results), an institution improves its result placement (Carnevale, 2005). Marketing administrators should work with their information technology unit to explore ways of improving search results and maximize potential benefits. Success on the Internet depends on attracting traffic and keeping it.

Digital Engagement

Digital engagement can be thought of as student engagement in the virtual world. In less than a generation, a whole new form of social networking and communication has emerged and changed the way people network and interact. Born and raised in an age of personal computers and the Internet, today's college students communicate through a variety of media. In addition to talking on cell phones, today's students are likely to e-mail each other, text message from cell phones or messaging programs, communicate through Web cams, send video messages and pictures, and leave messages on public "walls" or electronic bulletin boards.

Digital communication has made practices such as online social networking a true phenomenon. Beginning in the 1990s, the Internet brought a whole new medium of communication and connections between groups and individuals and expanded the notion of social networks. Message boards, e-mail, text messaging, file sharing, discussion groups, visual media, and blogging are the most popular modes of communication in this digital world and reflect a new culture of communication and the networks that support it.

Digital engagement, then, uses the new modes of communication, but it should not be seen as a substitute for traditional modes of communication or standard communication tools. Rather, it must function as a new tool with limited application, limited use, and limited expectations. The term "digital media" often implies limitless possibility, but admissions officers should regard digital communication the same way they regard tradition communication and not ascribe special powers to it. It is a niche communication tool that can be very effective but that has its limitations.

"Digital engagement" in this monograph is a catch-all term that includes e-mail, text messages, instant messaging, social networking (through Facebook and MySpace), and various forms of logs (Web logs, often called "blogs," video logs, and podcasts). Blogs and podcasts seem to be the most popular of these log communication tools, although their efficacy is largely debated. Admissions departments have been using e-mail for some time to communicate with applicants, but new tools are being used as well with varying levels of success (Farrell, 2007; Foster, 2003; Stoner, 2004).

The communication tools listed can be roughly broken into two groups, depending on their mode of communication. E-mail, text messages, and instant messaging represent active forms of communication; conversely, blogs, podcasts, and profiles on social networking are passive. Text messages and e-mail with deadline reminders and invitations to chat online are some of the ways institutions have begun to reach out to students (Stoner, 2004). Similarly, faculty, administrators, and students have been recruited to write about daily life on blogs, make podcasts available for downloading, and maintain profiles on social networking sites (Schevitz, 2007).

A report by Eduventures, Inc., entitled "College Search and the Millennial Generation," (2007) sheds light on how this generation of teenagers makes decisions about what school to attend. Results of a Web-based survey of 7,867 high school juniors and seniors and student feedback from twelve focus-group sessions indicate that 84 percent of survey respondents said they used college Web sites most often to research particular institutions, followed by personal recommendations (75 percent), campus visits (64 percent), and college viewbooks (64 percent).

The report also revealed important information about the social networking sites colleges and universities have been flocking to. With the popularity of Facebook, MySpace, and Second Life, colleges and universities have been creating institutional profiles to reach students where they live (Schevitz, 2007). Facebook and MySpace profiles are used as recruiting tools, with the institutions that create them hoping to communicate to potential students their relevance in a modern world. Some students report visiting college and university MySpace or Facebook pages as a way to communicate with current students at the institution or just to see the institutional profile available on social networking sites. One high school student commented to a reporter that he thought it was "pretty cool" to be able to see a school's profile on a social networking site. "I'm from the other side of the country, and it is good to be able to get an idea of what it is like to be there [in this case, San Francisco State University]. It is much easier than having to call the admissions office" (Schevitz, 2007, p. B3).

Although many schools have scrambled to have a presence on these sites, their efficacy is largely debatable, and the findings of "College Search and the Millennial Generation" bear that out. Chat rooms and blogs are not as popular as might be expected for a generation that is technologically savvy and proficient with online applications. Less than 10 percent of prospective college students use MySpace, Facebook, or YouTube as part of the search process, and the report concludes that official university Web sites are by far the most effective tool for reaching students.

For schools that intend to venture into online social networking or use other, more recent tools of communication, admissions deans report that they work best when current students and younger staff members are able to create the content and communicate with students. These campus personalities become a kind of "online college ambassador" through whom prospective students can be exposed to an institution and feel engaged—which is not to suggest that only young people can or should communicate to students through digital means. But it is important to involve them in the process to ensure the messages that are communicated are timely, relevant, and likely to appeal to the target audience. Carefully monitored reliance on younger staff and students to create content for digital communication is best for avoiding a dated, irrelevant message.

The goal for any of these communications tools is to be informative and create and sustain relationships, not to be intrusive or just another media message a person has to negotiate. Online communication is another way to make recruiting interactive and personal, but it risks alienating potential students. The last thing prospective students want is to be annoyed by unsolicited text messages and e-mail.

Expert opinions abound when it comes to how much communication should occur through online tools, but the consensus seems to be toward caution when entering the constantly evolving world of technology (Farrell, 2007; Foster, 2003; Stoner, 2004; Tedeschi, 2004). Some college recruiters warn that "dabbling in new media can prove expensive and time-consuming" and can create more work for admissions staff without "eliminating any of their old tasks" like answering inquiries or sending out printed materials (Adenekan, 2007).

Finally, a note about the power of the Internet for customers to communicate about their experiences. People can, and do, talk back today about their experiences with a company or, in our case, a college or university. Customers talk back through online reviews, blogs, and message boards. If they are upset or angry, they are much more likely to talk, and the power of search engines today makes it very easy for users to find what is being written. Customers now have power to communicate their dissatisfaction when they believe a company did not meet their expectations. Although the relationship a college or university has with its students and other key stakeholders is substantially different from the relationship United Airlines has with its passengers, the power of customer communication for both your school and United cannot be overstated. When people are dissatisfied, they often tell you. And they will likely tell each other, too.

You, too, can use the Web to your advantage. You have the power to see what people are saying about you. Search the Web; use those same powerful search engines to see what is being written about your institution and respond. Maybe some areas can be improved. Maybe someone will blog about an issue that currently resides in your organizational blind spot, and having light shed on it will make change possible. Although reading potentially unflattering things about your efforts can be difficult, it can also be constructive. Likewise, see what is being said about your competition. The Web is a powerful tool to learn about you and others. What you learn online could give you just the competitive advantage you need in the competitive world of student recruiting.

In this chapter the focus shifted from a discussion of how to make tangible the often intangible qualities of higher education to an examination of how institutional identity and branding are essential as one seeks to stand apart in a crowded marketplace. As we have seen, market differentiation in higher education involves communicating how an institution best suits consumers' needs and is the best choice of the available options. Different institutions accomplish this task differently, but it often involves communicating to multiple audiences the quality of the academic offerings and social and campus amenities and aligning the success of the athletic department with the rest of the institution. A professionally developed marketing plan that includes professionally designed promotional materials, viewbooks that reflect the institutional brand, and a digital presence that is geared toward communicating with a twenty-first-century audience is key to successful communication of what makes an institution stand apart from its competition.

Recommendations for Selling Higher Education

NO MONOGRAPH ON MARKETING AND ADVERTISING HIGHER EDUCATION would be complete without a section of recommendations. What follows are general marketing and advertising observations for business (as well as higher education), interspersed with recommendations targeted to colleges and universities. These observations and recommendations are by no means comprehensive, but they are presented to give you ideas about how best you might go about redesigning your marketing efforts or changing course in the face of increasing competition, declining enrollments, or a new marketing campaign.

These recommendations derive from basic market principles that make up the foundation of sound business marketing practice. They have been tested by countless businesses in a variety of fields, all trying to accomplish the same thing: persuading consumers to buy a product or service and then persuading them to repeat the action. And they work. How do we know? Because they have withstood the test of time; if capitalism teaches us one thing, it is that bad ideas do not last long in an open market. If these recommendations were not profitable, they would long have been forgotten.

As we have seen thus far, marketing and advertising the modern college or university are compounded by two forces, each working in concert to challenge even the best marketer. Higher education is an intangible product working for market differentiation in a crowded field. Moreover, higher education is sometimes a product, sometimes a service. The customers are students, but they are also the products. Colleges and universities are social institutions, but they are also forced to behave like modern businesses. Given all these factors, it is no wonder that Jugenheimer (1995) believes colleges and universities generally do a poor job of advertising and marketing. He cites several reasons contributing to this conclusion: inadequate planning, a general resistance to advertising (by academics and administrators alike), and the lack of a comprehensive marketing plan. Jugenheimer believes these poor marketing practices have their roots in the inexperience of administrators in advertising and marketing, as evidenced by research that reveals confusion among administrators about advertising terms used (Jugenheimer, 1995; Kittle, 2000) and about many marketing practices. Administrators often ascend from the faculty ranks and do not have the business degrees or marketing experience that would make them better suited for the demands of marketing higher education.

Compounded with this inexperience is the difficulty of marketing a college or university for all the reasons described in the opening of the preceding paragraph. And it does not help matters that very little research has been done on the actual practices of higher education institutional advertising (Kittle, 2000). We know institutions advertise and market themselves, but it is a highly underresearched area, making it difficult to implement empirically driven changes or strategies. Sometimes we just do not know why markets in higher education behave the way they do, and we have to make decisions based on the available data.

Despite these challenges, we do know that marketing and advertising higher education are about understanding the "product," defining the central message, and creating memorable images that an audience can associate with the particular college or university. Although the field of marketing higher education is relatively new, much has been written about general market research techniques to measure image, and advice abounds about how to create or improve an image so that it contributes to a "unified marketing plan" (Topor, 1986).

Marketing higher education should be thought of as a two-step approach with two clear objectives:

Create a positive common image that is easy to communicate to all audiences. It could include a common logo, a slogan, or some other identifying characteristic that is exclusive to your institutional brand. Brand status is not likely to happen overnight, but it is possible to develop a common image that faculty, staff, students, and alumni recognize and promote. A brand community depends on a common core for identification, something to rally around.

Within your common image, communicate distinct images for the variety of target audiences you wish to reach: current and prospective students, parents, alumni, faculty and staff, donors, the community (local, regional, national), legislators, and the media. Each niche market expects different things from your institution; you should research and identify their expectations so you have an appeal that reaches their needs.

Kittle's research (2000) into advertising practices has found that most institutions use all major media and that "communication objectives most often mentioned were general image enhancement and awareness of the institution" (p. 37).

Image and awareness should be at the core of your efforts, regardless of the media used for advertising purposes or your institutional type. According to Newman's study (2002), which measured the current state of marketing in higher education, "Nearly all of the marketing and planning activities included in the study were consistently practiced across the various types of institutions in the United States," lending support "to the assertion that the practice of marketing is not substantially affected by the differentiated structure of higher education" (p. 25). Although theory and existing research suggest that "institution size, funding type, and innovativeness have significant impacts on the market orientation of higher education" (Wasmer and Bruner, 1999, p. 104), it need not prevent a wide assortment of media venues or the content of messages. Be open-minded about the media available to you and the types of messages you create and disseminate. Creativity is hard to ignore.

Collaborative Partners

Higher education is not business, and the distinction is important. Bay and Daniel (2001) write that the fundamental differences between higher education and business also preclude "the customer-focus" so prevalent in the business literature "from being an entirely useful one" when applied to marketing strategies of higher education (p. 1). "In fact," they write, "the student-as-a-customer paradigm may cause institutions to concentrate on short-term, narrow student satisfaction, rather than meeting the long-term needs of an entire range of stakeholders" (p. 1). Bay and Daniel propose that the student be regarded as a "collaborative partner" rather than as a customer or consumer of higher education. They believe an institution—student collaborative partnership allows for the different kinds of relationships that exist between the institution and the student.

This concept is sound, and using the term "collaborative partners" addresses the issues many academicians have regarding higher education as a "business" with "customers" who must be satisfied, regardless of the effort required to do so. Higher education is a complicated business. Sometimes the student is a customer buying living space or meals or shopping at the bookstore and using various facilities on campus (Bay and Daniel, 2001). Other times the student is a learner or the product of education. Regardless, students' roles and their relationship to the university are dynamic and cannot be reduced to a customer-business paradigm alone. Further, a collaborative partnership recognizes that each party brings something that benefits the other in a "complex, evolving" relationship (p. 8). To stay vital, the partnership must grow and evolve.

The orientation toward collaborative partnerships is also critical because students represent a difficult market for colleges and universities. Litten (1980) claims that "the most problematic set of consumers for the responsive marketer is the traditional prospective student—the high school senior. . . . A young person graduating from high school frequently knows only vaguely what educational benefits he or she wants and only a little about what he or she needs" (p. 88). Students are not traditional customers with specific needs or expectations. They are often confused about what exactly they are looking for, but they also recognize the decision they will make will have great influence over the rest of their lives.

Of the choice process, Galotti and Kozberg (1996) write that students understand their choice is, "in several ways, life framing," and they "recognize the fact that the college decision is one of great magnitude, with many ramifications for career and family choices" (p. 3). The magnitude of the decision, the complexity of the choices, and their uncertainty about what they need lead to great parental involvement for many prospective students. As such, parents should be considered key elements in the collaborative partnership. "By the senior year, parents have played a key, if subliminal, role in establishing constraints on students' consideration sets" (Hossler, Schmit, and Vesper, 1999, p. 133). Therefore, marketing should be directed to parents as much as to students.

Clinton (1989) echoes this sentiment when he advises that promotional efforts:

- Be directed to parents as well as potential students;
- Include parental figures and peers in promotional materials, as they weigh heavily in the choice process;
- Be designed with a friendly atmosphere that is inviting and inclusive;
- Stress quality of education for the cost; and
- Mention a good track record of prompt responses to inquiries and early notification of acceptance, as both significantly increase enrollments.

McDonough, Antonio, and Horvat (1996) have demonstrated that students make a college choice based on the advice of family and school personnel, their perceptions of key anticipated social experiences, and what they perceive as the ability to convert their college degree into a job or advanced education. Marketing efforts should be targeted with these considerations in mind but recognize they are not mutually exclusive. Marketers are advised that college choice is grounded in "a sort of holistic pragmatism" and that "final choice is likely to be based as much on a feeling of well-being, or at least a lack of discomfort, as on any rational calculation of costs and benefits or systematic ratings of institutional characteristics" (Litten, 1991, p. 132)— which explains the conclusion Karp, Holmstrom, and Gray (1998) reach when they write, "It is not especially surprising that one of the most consistent and universal patterns in our data is the effort expended by students to find a school where 'a person like me will feel comfortable'" (p. 275).

The search for a good fit often comes down to the campus visit. The literature is clear that the campus visit creates a personal contact in what has been, until then, a fairly impersonal relationship. The campus visit is literally a handshake and a welcome. It is the campus visit where the student experiences what has largely been an abstraction and allows them to test the assumptions they have carried based on their other information channels (print materials, online information, and others' perceptions). Campus visits represent an important factor in student choice that "can be changed more easily than the number of majors offered or the location of the school. Consequently, it offers enormous potential as a recruiting tool" (Rosen, Curran, and Greenlee, 1998, p. 90). Finally, Clinton (1989) believes campus tours should be conducted by selected college students who embody the characteristics a campus hopes to promote. "Fears of the unknown are quickly dissolved with a friendly campus tour" (p. 40).

Strategic Marketing Plans for Higher Education

If you want to be successful in marketing, think like a marketer. Marketers who are successful think strategically about two things: the product and the market. The first step toward marketing higher education is to establish a strategic marketing plan that considers two overarching concerns: (1) your position in the competitive marketplace and (2) how you will implement and support your strategy on a day-to-day basis (Hiebing and Cooper, 1997; Kotler, 1999; Kotler and Keller, 2006). It is essential that a college or university know what it is, whom it serves, and who the competition is. Likewise, it is important that the day-to-day operations, including budgets and personnel, be able to support the market strategy that is created. Having an extensive plan with no means to support it is pointless.

A strategic marketing plan begins with a marketing audit, which is a tool for analyzing an institution's internal strengths and weaknesses and matching them with external opportunities and threats (Goldgehn, 1990). Simply put, a marketing audit is a self-assessment applied to the market. It asks what you do well and to articulate your strengths and cite evidence to support what makes you strong in those particular areas. Likewise, it asks you to evaluate your weaknesses, both relative and by comparison. Are you able to identify external opportunities in the market that you currently use and those you could better exploit? What about your threats? Who are your competitors, both immediate and distant?

The ability to classify strengths and weaknesses and to assess opportunities and threats satisfies what Sands and Smith (1999) believe is key to organizational effectiveness that communicates a strong identity: the development of an effective market and communications plan that "melds the capability to . . . effectively respond to those opportunities identified through an integrated marketing effort" (p. 41). Although true integration is a lofty goal, Sands and Smith contend it is critical in "today's noisy marketplace because the more integrated and consistent an institution's marketing and communications activities are, the more likely it is to realize significant gains in its visibility and reputation" (p. 42).

Successful market orientation requires innovative ideas. Organizational culture that supports good internal communication polices and internal marketing practices is more likely to foster organizational values that promote innovative practice (Wasmer and Bruner, 1999), of which marketing and strategic planning can be a major part. Marketing orientation that is clearly communicated and accepted across an organization's central units is most likely to communicate values that are at the core of the institution's identity and can then be communicated to external audiences.

The process by which prospective students arrive at a decision to attend a college or university varies substantially, but certain actions that students take demonstrate their interest and eventual decision regarding enrollment (Capraro, Patrick, and Wilson 2004; Coccari and Javalgi, 1995; Kallio, 1995)— requesting more information, visiting campus, and applying for admission (Capraro, Patrick, and Wilson, 2004). Your marketing plan should follow them every step of the way as you anticipate their needs, answer their questions, respond to their needs, and demonstrate your good fit.

Relationship Marketing

Relationship marketing emphasizes building long-term relationships with customers rather than focusing on each individual transaction (Berry, 1995, 2002; Gordon, 1998; Jackson, 1982). It involves understanding customers' needs over a long period of time; as they change, so too do their needs. Business needs to be responsive to these changing needs and offer a range of products or services to existing customers as needed.

Fundamentally, relationship marketing is the concept that "the purpose of a business is to create and keep a customer" (Levitt, 1986, p. 19). According to

Berry (1995), relationship marketing examines the relationship between the business that is being marketed and the customer that is being marketed to in an effort to earn and retain customer loyalty by fostering a long-term relationship. One method of examining this relationship is to provide opportunities for feedback from customers and potential customers (Normann, 1991).

Relationship marketing is an ongoing process of "identifying and creating new value with individual customers and then sharing the benefits from [it] over a lifetime of association" (Gordon, 1998, p. 18). According to Kittle and Ciba (1997), doing so encourages colleges and universities to "attract students, help them graduate, assist them in their careers, and seek their moral and financial support for the rest of their lives" (p. 19). Thus, institutions must employ a wide range of marketing techniques to communicate to their various market audiences that what they seek is a relationship, not simply a business transaction. Colleges and universities have an advantage over online higher education providers in that they bring the power of a social institution and the cultures that swirl around campus experiences to forge true partnerships with students, alumni, and supporters. They must recognize this power in their relationships with their various audiences.

The most enduring benefits of relationship marketing "come from identifying the relationships members of the university community value, and providing for the experiential contexts in which they can be formed" (McAlexander, Koenig, and Schouten, 2004, p. 77), which helps to explain why rallying around the team works so well as a manifestation of that branded community.

Relationship marketing applies directly to the consumer engagement needs of higher education. Colleges and universities are big places that often do not have a good sense of themselves or what they do. When the organizational mission is clearly defined and articulated, people respond. They want a clear mission and vision. They want to know what the organization is about and how they fit in. Marketing provides a vehicle for a college or university to define what it does and for whom. Each part works together instead of in isolation. A new marketing campaign is an opportunity for everyone to see how he or she fits into the larger institution, who the customers are, and how the organization can address customers' needs across their lifetime.

The ultimate goal of relationship marketing as applied to higher education is for institutions to:

1. Communicate who they are and what they have to offer to their market audiences. No market audience should question how it personally relates to the institution; the relationship should be explicit.
2. Address the individual needs of their market audiences as appropriate. For example, prospective students, current students, and alumni all have different relationships with an institution; care must be taken to communicate to each audience that the institution understands its needs.
3. Fulfill their promises. Expectations have been set and should be met. Not meeting expectations will cause market audiences to question the quality of the relationship and the institutions.

By taking these steps, institutions have an opportunity to build a base of loyal and committed partners who understand the institution and how they fit in it and are likely to remain in the relationship for a long time.

Importance of Internal Marketing

Relationship marketing largely depends on successful internal marketing for an organization. Internal marketing is simply the act of using marketing techniques in the institution itself to enhance the organizational relationships among employees, departments, and leaders (George, 1990). If things work as they should, each person working in the organization gives and receives positive services in their interactions with one another, and, it is hoped, this positive interaction is communicated to external audiences. George (1990) writes that it works best when those working in the organization understand the significance of their own roles as well as the role and significance of others. An effective internal marketing program is thought to be essential for external marketing efforts, as each person understands customer needs from the customer's perspective as well as the organization's mission, vision, and goals.

The goal for marketing your particular institution is to communicate to all members of the organization what your institutional priorities are and how each individual plays a role in advancing your collective mission. Successful marketing in higher education begins internally. Discuss your goals, develop your strategy, communicate your message, and be sure it all begins at home.

Branding is most successful when it involves many facets of marketing such as use of slogans and logo design but also when it is consistent across the organization and provides a common image that brand communities can attach themselves to as an expression of their loyalty. A clear brand image functions as a relationship builder between individual members of the community and further binds them to the institution, both as individuals but also as separate communities that share the institution in common. Difficulties often accompany efforts to market an intangible product, which points to the importance of "branding" as a critical component of image construction. Branding creates a clear message about an intangible product and helps to build awareness and relevance in an often crowded marketplace. This factor is especially important as colleges and universities struggle to stand out, or even to be noticed, in a crowded marketplace.

Ultimately, the marketing goal for colleges and universities should be twofold: (1) make the intangible tangible and (2) find areas of market differentiation. When considering the intangible nature of education, marketing researchers (see, for example, Johnson and Sallee, 1994; Kotler and Armstrong, 1996) suggest asking what evidence you can offer that reflects who you are and what you do as an institution. The key here is *evidence*. What can you point to and say, "See that? *That* is what we do"? Because the "results of education, such as knowledge, values, ethics, and skills are hard to conceptualize . . . admissions professionals must find and supply tangible evidence that successfully distinguishes their institution from all others" (Johnson and Sallee, 1994, p. 16).

Summary and Conclusions

TO BE VIABLE IN THE MODERN ERA, today's colleges and universities must strike a balance between advancing the public trust as social institutions and places of higher learning while also being aware of the contemporary challenges of running large organizations with dwindling public support and greater competition from the for-profit sector. Zemsky, Wegner, and Massy (2005) call it being "market-smart and mission-centered," a construct supported by Canterbury (1999), who recommends a concept of higher education that is "product as opportunity" rather than a flat designation that is just product.

Observing colleges and universities from this perspective allows one to see how the current higher education market both supports and propels the mission rather than obstructing it. Successful marketing of colleges and universities, then, aims to be both mission driven *and* market driven. The institution and those charged with running it are obligated to be attentive to the market and employ sound marketing practices to determine current market demands and how to address, deliver, and satisfy them. One could even argue that an institution needs to be not only market driven but also market *savvy*. Market savvy repositions the organization and shifts control to the institution. Rather than simply being responsive to the market, a market-savvy organization anticipates needs and change and adapts and prepares accordingly.

Colleges and universities offer largely intangible experiences that are difficult to quantify, measure, and evaluate, which explains why so much of what emanates from marketing and advertising follows the "peripheral route" of persuasion in the Elaboration Likelihood Model. When applied to higher education, this peripheral route messaging clarifies college and university efforts to advertise and highlight elements of the college experience that have little to do with the process of learning itself. The appeal is peripheral, not central, because the central route or message is too similar across institutions. The institutional similarity and cluttered environment are complicated by the need for market differentiation, marketing a largely intangible product, and having to rely on emotional connections and brand communities for customer loyalties. Most colleges and universities offer similar central features (similar curricula, similar housing, and so forth) in their respective institutional classifications. And they therefore rely on peripheral characteristics and an emotional response from the audiences they are trying to persuade to take action on their message.

Colleges and universities that are not only aware of this environment but also are savvy about the changing marketplace increase their chances of establishing distinction among their peers. College choice for the college bound is a complicated process that involves many variables and many influential parties throughout the process. Colleges and universities that can be responsive to needs and proactive in communicating features about their core mission and identity and their many offerings thrive. Strong institutional identity requires clearly recognizing one's organizational strengths, effectively communicating how one is different in a crowded marketplace, and building collaborative partnerships internally and externally to promote greater awareness and recognition among key stakeholders. Strategic marketing enables one to move from being simply *driven* by the market to being *savvy* about it.

Arthur Levine observed that colleges and universities are becoming more individualized, as students, not institutions, are setting the educational agenda. He predicts that in a twenty-first-century higher education environment, "Each student will be able to choose from a multitude of knowledge providers, the form of instruction, and the courses most consistent with how he or she learns" (2000, p. B10). That reality is now. As we make our way deeper into the new realities of higher education, we are embarking on an era marked by dwindling support and increased competition; it is incumbent on administrators and higher education leaders at colleges and universities to broadcast who they are, what they do, and what makes them valuable. The business of higher education depends on it.

References

Aaker, D. A. (1991). *Managing brand equity.* New York: Free Press.

Aaker, D. A. (2000). *Managing brand equity: Capitalizing on the value of a brand name.* Chicago: Free Press.

Adelman, C. (2006). How to design a web site that welcomes prospective applicants. *Chronicle of Higher Education, 53*(10), B26.

Adenekan, S. (2007, April 27). MySpace: The final frontier. *Education Guardian.* Retrieved September, 13, 2007, from http://www.guardian.co.uk/education/2007/apr/27/highereducation.accesstouniversity

Agres, S. J., Edell, J. A., and Dubitsky, T. M. (1990). *Emotion in advertising: Theoretical and practical explorations.* New York: Quorum Books.

Andre, J., and James, D. N. (1991). *Rethinking college athletics.* Philadelphia: Temple University Press.

Armstrong, J. J., and Lumsden, D. B. (1999). Impact on universities' promotional materials on college choice. *Journal of Marketing for Higher Education, 9*(2), 83–91.

Arnoldy, B. (2007, April 12). College presidents plan "U.S. News" rankings boycott. *Christian Science Monitor,* A6.

Baade, R. A., and Sundberg, J. O. (1996). Fourth down and gold to go? Assessing the link between athletics and alumni giving. *Social Science Quarterly, 77*(2), 790–803.

Backer, H. W., Spielvogel, J. J., and Bates, R. (1991). A paradox? A paradox! A most ingenious paradox! *Currents, 2,* 1–7.

Baker, W. E. (1999). When can affective conditioning and mere exposure directly influence brand choice? *Journal of Advertising, 28*(4), 31–47.

Bartlett, T. (2007, Nov. 23). Your (lame) slogan here. *Chronicle of Higher Education, 54*(13), A1.

Bauerly, R. J., and Tripp, C. (1997). Developing slogans for marketing of higher education. *Journal of Marketing for Higher Education, 8*(1), 1–14.

Bay, D., and Daniel, H. (2001). The student is not the customer: An alternative perspective. *Journal of Marketing for Higher Education, 11*(1), 1–19.

Berry, L. (1995). Relationship marketing of services: Growing interest, emerging perspectives. *Journal of the Academy of Marketing Science, 23*(4), 236–245.

Berry, L. (2002). Relationship marketing of services: Perspectives from 1983 and 2000. *Journal of Relationship Marketing, 1*(1), 59–77.

Best, R. (2004). *Market-based management* (4th ed.). Upper Saddle River, NJ: Prentice Hall.

Bierley, C., McSweeney, F. K., and Vannieuwkerk, R. (1985). Classical conditioning of preferences for stimuli. *Journal of Consumer Research, 12*(3), 316.

Blackscon, M. (1992). Observations: Building brand equity by managing the brand's relationship. *Journal of Advertising Research, 32*(3), 79–83.

Blumenstyk, G. (2006). Marketing, the for-profit way. *Chronicle of Higher Education, 53*(15), A20.

Bok, D. (2003). *Universities in the marketplace: The commercialization of higher education.* Princeton, NJ: Princeton University Press.

Bornstein, R. F. (1989). Exposure and affect: Overview and meta-analysis of research, 1968-1987. *Psychological Bulletin, 106*(2), 265–289.

Boyer, P. (2003). *College rankings exposed: The art of getting a quality education in the 21st century.* Lawrenceville, NJ: Peterson's.

Brock, T. C. (1967). Communication discrepancy and intent to persuade as determinants of counterargument production. *Journal of Experimental Social Psychology, 3,* 269–309.

Broekemier, G. M., and Seshadri, S. (1999). Differences in college choice criteria between deciding students and their parents. *Journal of Marketing for Higher Education, 9*(3), 1–13.

Cabrera, A. F., and La Nasa, S. M. (2000). *Understanding the college-choice process.* New Directions for Institutional Research, no. 107, pp. 5–22. San Francisco: Jossey-Bass.

Canterbury, R. M. (1999). Higher education marketing: A challenge. *Journal of College Admission, 165,* 22–30.

Capraro, A. J., Patrick, M. L., and Wilson, M. (2004). Attracting college candidates: The impact of perceived social life. *Journal of Marketing for Higher Education, 14*(1), 93–106.

Carlson, S. (2003). Marshall U. will offer cell phones, not traditional phones, in 4 dorms. *Chronicle of Higher Education, 49*(30), A35.

Carnevale, D. (2005). To size up colleges, students now shop online. *Chronicle of Higher Education, 51*(40), A25.

Chapman, D. W. (1981). A model of student college choice. *Journal of Higher Education, 52*(5), 490–505.

Chressanthis, G. A., and Grimes, P. W. (1993). Intercollegiate success and first-year student enrollment demands. *Sociology of Sport Journal, 10*(3), 286–300.

Chu, D. (1989). *The character of American higher education and intercollegiate sport.* Albany: State University of New York Press.

Chute, E. (2006, April 2). Home and away: College-bound kids don't stray far from home. *Pittsburgh Post-Gazette,* B1.

Clinton, R. J. (1989). Factors that influence the college prospect's choice of schools: Methodology, analysis and marketing implications of a recent study. *Journal of Marketing for Higher Education, 2*(2), 31–45.

Cobb-Walgren, C. J., Ruble, C. A., and Donthu, N. (1995). Brand equity, brand preference, and purchase intent. *Journal of Advertising, 24*(3), 25–40.

Coccari, R. L., and Javalgi, R. G. (1995). Analysis of students' needs in selecting a college or university in a changing environment. *Journal of Marketing for Higher Education, 6*(2), 27–39.

Cohen, A. M. (1998). *The shaping of American higher education: Emergence and growth of the contemporary system.* San Francisco: Jossey-Bass.

College Board. (2008). *The College Board college handbook 2008.* New York: College Board.

Conard, M. J., and Conard, M. A. (2000). An analysis of academic reputation as perceived by consumers of higher education. *Journal of Marketing for Higher Education, 9*(4), 69–80.

Conklin, M. E., and Dailey, A. R. (1981). Does consistency of parental encouragement matter for secondary students? *Sociology of Education, 54,* 254–262.

Cox, J., and Dale, B. G. (2002). Key quality factors in web site design and use: An examination. *International Journal of Quality & Reliability Management, 19*(7), 862–888.

Dahlin-Brown, N. (2005). The perceptual impact of *U.S. News and World Report* rankings on eight public MBA programs. *Journal of Marketing for Higher Education, 15*(2), 155–179.

Day, G. S. (1999). *Market driven strategy: Processes for creating value.* New York: Free Press.

Dillon, S. (2006, Sept. 26). Secretary vows to improve results of higher education. *New York Times,* 20.

Doherty, T. (2002). DVD PDQ. *Chronicle of Higher Education (Chronicle Review),* B15.

Dowling, G. R. (1988). Measuring corporate images: A review of alternative approaches. *Journal of Business Research, 17,* 27–34.

Duderstadt, J. J. (2000). *Intercollegiate athletics and the American university.* Ann Arbor: University of Michigan Press.

Edmondson, B. (1987). Colleges conquer the baby bust. *American Demographics, 55*(9), 27–31.

Eduventures, Inc. (2007). *College search and the millennial generation.* Available from http://www.eduventures.com.

Farquhar, P. H. (1989). Managing brand equity. *Marketing Research, 1,* 24–33.

Farrell, C. (1989). Historical overview. In R. E. Lapchick and J. B. Slaughter (Eds.), *The rules of the game: Ethics in college sports* (pp. 21–39). New York: American Council on Education & Macmillan Publishing Company.

Farrell, E. F. (2007). Tangled up in tech: Admissions deans grapple with the promises and pitfalls of electronic recruiting. *Chronicle of Higher Education, 53*(28), A36.

Farrell, E. F., and Van Der Werf, M. (2007). Playing the rankings game. *Chronicle of Higher Education, 53*(38), A11.

Fiske, E. (2008). *Fiske Guide to Colleges 2008.* Naperville, IL: Sourcebooks, Inc.

Foster, A. L. (2003). Colleges find more applicants through personalized web recruiting. *Chronicle of Higher Education, 49*(34), A37.

Foster, A., and Carnevale, D. (2007). Looking to make money and reach more working students, state universities are pushing into the U. of Phoenix's territory. *Chronicle of Higher Education, 53*(34), A49.

Fram, E. H. (1982). *Maintaining and enhancing a college or university image.* Rochester, NY: Institute of Technology.

Frederickson, H. G. (2001, Jan./Feb.). Getting ranked. *Change,* 49–55.

Furbeck, L. F. (2003). A, B, CD, DVD: Marketing higher education to the millennial generation. *Journal of Marketing for Higher Education, 13*(1/2), 17–31.

Galotti, K. M., and Kozberg, S. F. (1996). Adolescents' experience of a life-framing decision. *Journal of Youth and Adolescence, 25,* 3–16.

Gaski, J. F., and Etzel, M. J. (1984). Collegiate athletic success and alumni generosity: Dispelling the myth. *Social Behavior and Personality, 12*(1), 29–38.

George, W. (1990). Internal marketing and organizational behavior. *Journal of Business Research, 20*(1), 145–152.

Goldgehn, L. A. (1990). Are U.S. colleges and universities applying marketing techniques properly and within the context of an overall marketing plan? *Journal of Marketing for Higher Education, 3*(1), 39–53.

Gordon, I. (1998). *Relationship marketing: New strategies, techniques and technologies to win the customers you want and keep them forever.* Toronto, Ontario: John Wiley & Sons Canada.

Gose, B. (2000, May 5). The theories of college marketing go only so far at some colleges. *Chronicle of Higher Education,* A50.

Gose, B. (2006). Juggling the costs of campus "amenities" when students help decide what to spend. *Chronicle of Higher Education, 52*(21), B10.

Greenwald, A. G. (1968). On defining attitude and attitude theory. In A. G. Greenwald, T. C. Brock, and T. M. Ostrom, (Eds.), *Psychological foundation of attitude* (pp. 65–111). New York: Academic Press.

Greenwald, B. (2001, Mar. 21). 'Flutie factor' still in contention. *The Chronicle* (Duke University Student Newspaper), A7.

Gumport, P. (2000). Academic restructuring: Organizational change and institutional imperatives. *Higher Education 39*(1), 67–91.

Hanford, G. (1974). *An inquiry into the need for the feasibility of a national study of intercollegiate athletics.* Washington, DC: American Council on Education.

Hansmann, H. (1980). The rationale for exempting nonprofit organizations from corporate income taxation. *Yale Law Journal, 91,* 54–100.

Hayes, D., and Wynyard, R. (Eds.). (2002). *The McDonaldization of higher education.* Westport, CT: Bergin & Garvey.

Henderson, A. T., and Berla, N. (1994). *A new generation of evidence: The family is critical on student achievement.* Washington, DC: National Committee for Citizens in Education.

Hesel, R. A. (2004). Know thyself: Five strategies for marketing a college. *Chronicle of Higher Education, 50*(34), B9.

Hiebing, R. G., and Cooper, S. W. (1997). *The successful marketing plan: A disciplined and comprehensive approach.* Chicago: VGM Career Books.

Hite, R. E., and Yearwood, A. (2001). A content analysis of college and university viewbooks (brochures). *College and University, 76*(3), 17–21.

Hossler, D., Braxton, J., and Coopersmith, G. (1989). Understanding student college choice. In J. C. Smart (Ed.), *Higher education: Handbook of theory and research* (Vol. 5). New York: Agathon.

Hossler, D., and Gallagher, K. S. (1987). Studying student college choice: A three-phase model and the implications for policy-makers. *College and University 2*(3), 207–221.

Hossler, D., Schmit, J., and Vesper, N. (1999). *Going to college: How social, economic, and educational factors influence the decisions students make.* Baltimore: Johns Hopkins University Press.

Hossler, D., and Vesper, N. (1993). An exploratory study of the factors associated with parental saving for postsecondary education. *Journal of Higher Education, 64*(2), 140–165.

Jackson, G. A. (1982). Public efficiency and private choice in higher education. *Education Evaluation and Policy Analysis, 4*(2), 237–247.

Johnson, J., and Sallee, D. (1994). Marketing your college as an intangible product. *Journal of College Admission, 144,* 16–20.

Jugenheimer, D. W. (1995). Advertising the university: A professional approach to promoting the college or university. *Journal of Marketing for Higher Education, 6*(1), 1–22.

Kallio, R. (1995). Factors influencing the college choice decisions of graduate students. *Research in Higher Education, 36*(1), 109–124.

Karp, D. A., Holmstrom, L. L., and Gray, P. S. (1998). Leaving home for college: Expectations for selective reconstruction of self. *Symbolic Interaction, 21,* 253–276.

Katz, M., and Rose, J. (1969). Is your slogan identifiable? *Journal of Advertising Research, 9*(1), 21–26.

Keller, G. (1983). *Academic strategy: The management revolution in American higher education.* Baltimore: Johns Hopkins University Press.

Kellogg, A. P. (2001, Oct. 19). Facing more, and possibly pickier, students, colleges renovate and add housing. *Chronicle of Higher Education,* A37.

Kellogg Commission on the Future of State and Land-Grant Universities. (1999, February). Returning to our roots: The engaged institution. An open letter to the presidents and chancellors of state universities and land-grant colleges.

Kinser, K. (2006). *From Main Street to Wall Street: The transformation of for-profit higher education.* ASHE Higher Education Report, no. 31(5). San Francisco: Jossey-Bass.

Kirp, D. L. (2003). *Shakespeare, Einstein, and the bottom line: The marketing of higher education.* Cambridge, MA: Harvard University Press.

Kittle, B. (2000). Institutional advertising in higher education. *Journal of Marketing for Higher Education, 9*(4), 37–52.

Kittle, B. (2001). Using college web sites for student recruitment: A relationship marketing study. *Journal of Marketing for Higher Education, 11*(3), 17–37.

Kittle, B., and Ciba, D. (1997). Relationship marketing in higher education via the World Wide Web: An analysis of home pages examining student recruitment strategies. In *1997 Symposium for the Marketing of Higher Education Proceedings, American Marketing Association* (pp. 166–175). Chicago: American Marketing Association.

Klassen, M. L. (2000). Lots of fun, not much work, and no hassles: Marketing images of higher education. *Journal of Marketing for Higher Education, 10*(2), 11–26.

Kotler, P. (1999). *Kotler on marketing: How to create, win, and dominate markets.* New York: Free Press.

Kotler, P., and Armstrong, G. (1996). *Principles of marketing.* Englewood Cliffs, NJ: Prentice Hall.

Kotler, P., and Fox, K.F.A. (1995). *Strategic marketing for educational institutions.* Englewood Cliffs, NJ: Prentice Hall.

Kotler, P., and Keller, K. L. (2006). *Marketing management* (12th ed.). Upper Saddle River, NJ: Prentice Hall.

Krachenberg, A. R. (1972). Bringing the concept of marketing to higher education. *Journal of Higher Education, 43,* 369–380.

Krugman, D. M., Reid, L. N., Dunn, S. W., and Barban, A. M. (1994). *Advertising: Its role in modern marketing.* Fort Worth, TX: Dryden Press.

Krugman, H. E. (1965). The impact of television advertising: Learning without involvement. *Public Opinion Quarterly, 29*(3), 349–356.

Landrum, R., Turrisi, R., and Harless, C. (1998). University image: The benefits of assessment and modeling. *Journal of Marketing for Higher Education, 9*(1), 53–68.

Lawrence, P. R. (1987). *Unsportsmanlike conduct: The National Collegiate Athletic Association and the business of college football.* New York: Praeger.

Leuthesser, L., Kohli, C. S., and Harich, K. R. (1995). Brand equity: The halo effect measure. *European Journal of Marketing, 29*(4), 57–66.

Levine, A. E. (2000, Oct. 27). The future of colleges: 9 inevitable changes. *Chronicle of Higher Education,* B10.

Levitt, T. (1986). *The marketing imagination.* London: Collier Macmillan.

Litten, L. H. (1980). Marketing higher education: A reappraisal. In *Marketing in college admissions: A broadening perspective.* New York: College Board.

Litten, L. H. (1982). Different strokes in the applicant pool: Some refinements in a model of student college choice. *Journal of Higher Education, 53*(4), 383–402.

Litten, L. H. (1991). *Ivy bound: High-ability students and college choice.* New York: College Board.

Maguire, J. (2001, May 4). Applicants like winning teams [Letter to the editor]. *Chronicle of Higher Education,* B18.

Mallette, B. I. (1995). *Money Magazine, U.S. News and World Report,* and Steve Martin: What do they have in common? In R. D. Walleri and M. K. Moss (Eds.), *Evaluating and responding to college guidebooks and rankings.* San Francisco: Jossey-Bass.

Manski, C. F., and Wise, D. A. (1983). *College choice in America.* Cambridge, MA: Harvard University Press.

Martin, D. N. (1989). *Romancing the brand: The power of advertising and how to use it.* New York: Amacom Books.

McAlexander, J. H., Koenig, H. F., and Schouten, J. W. (2004). Building a university brand community: The long-term impact of shared experiences. *Journal of Marketing for Higher Education, 14*(2), 61–79.

McAlexander, J. H., Schouten, J. W., and Koenig, H. J. (2002). Building brand community. *Journal of Marketing, 66,* 38–54.

McCarthy, J. E. (1960). *Basic marketing: A managerial approach.* Homewood, IL: R. D. Irwin.

McCormack, E. (2005). A battle of inches. *Chronicle of Higher Education, 51*(33), A6.

McCormick, R. E., and Tinsley, M. (1990). Athletics versus academics: A model of university contributions. In B. L. Goff and R. D. Tollinson (Eds.), *Sportometics* (pp. 1193–1204). College Station: Texas A&M University Press.

McDonough, P. M., Antonio, A. L., and Horvat, E. M. (1996, August). *College choice as capital conversion and investment: A new model.* Paper presented at a meeting of the American Sociological Association, New York, NY.

Muniz, A., and O'Guinn, T. (2001). Brand communities. *Journal of Consumer Research, 27*(4), 412–432.

Neustadt, M. S. (1994, Winter). Is marketing good for higher education? *Journal of College Admission,* 17–22.

Newman, C. M. (2002). The current state of marketing activity among higher education institutions. *Journal of Marketing for Higher Education, 12*(1), 15–29.

Nord, W. R., and Peter, J. P. (1980). A behavior modification perspective on marketing. *Journal of Marketing, 44*(1), 36–47.

Normann, R. (1991). *Service management: Strategy and leadership in service business* (3rd ed.). New York: Wiley.

Parameswaran, R., and Glowacka, A. E. (1995). University image: An information processing perspective. *Journal of Marketing for Higher Education, 6*(2), 41–56.

Parker, R. S., Schaefer, A. D., Matthews, L., and Zammuto, R. F. (1996). The marketing of residence halls: A question of positioning. *Journal of Marketing for Higher Education, 7*(1), 33–44.

Pearson, S. (1996). *Building brands directly: Creating business value from customer relationships.* New York: NYU Press.

Pendergrast, M. (2000). *For God, country, and Coca-Cola: The definitive history of the great American soft drink and the company that makes it.* New York: Basic Books.

Perloff, R. M. (2003). *The dynamics of persuasion: Communication and attitudes in the 21st century* (2nd ed.). Mahwah, NJ: Erlbaum.

Petty, R. E., and Cacioppo, J. T. (1981). *Attitudes and persuasion: Classic and contemporary approaches.* Dubuque, IA: Wm. C. Brown.

Petty, R. E., and Cacioppo, J. T. (1984a). The effects of involvement on response to argument quantity and quality: Central and peripheral routes to persuasion. *Journal of Personality and Social Psychology, 46,* 69–81.

Petty, R. E., and Cacioppo, J. T. (1984b). Source factors and the elaboration likelihood model of persuasion. *Advances in Consumer Research, 11,* 668–672.

Petty, R. E., and Cacioppo, J. T. (1986a). *Communication and persuasion: Central and peripheral routes to persuasion.* New York: Springer-Verlag.

Petty, R. E., and Cacioppo, J. T. (1986b). The elaboration likelihood model of persuasion. In L. Berkowitz (Ed.), *Advances in experimental social psychology, 19,* 123–205. New York: Academic Press.

Petty, R. E., Ostrom, T. M., and Brock, T. C. (Eds.). (1981). *Cognitive responses in persuasion.* Hillsdale, NJ: Erlbaum.

Princeton Review. (2008a). *America's best value colleges, 2008 Edition.* New York: Princeton Review.

Princeton Review. (2008b). *The best 366 colleges, 2008 Edition.* New York: Princeton Review.

Princeton Review. (2008c). *Complete book of colleges, 2008 Edition.* New York: Princeton Review.

Pulley, J. L. (2003). Romancing the brand. *Chronicle of Higher Education, 50*(9), A30.

Ramasubramanian, S., Gyure, J. F., and Mursi, N. M. (2002). Impact of Internet images: Impression-formation effects of university web site images. *Journal of Marketing for Higher Education, 12*(2), 59–68.

Ray, M. L., Sawyer, A. G., Rothschild, M. L., Heeler, M. R., and Reed, J. B. (1973). Marketing communications and the hierarchy of effects. In P. Clarke (Ed.), *New Models for Mass Communication Research.* Beverly Hills, CA: Sage.

Rhoades, F.H.T. (2006). After 40 years of growth and change, higher education faces new challenges. *Chronicle of Higher Education, 53*(14), A18.

Rhoads, T. A., and Gerking, S. (2000). Educational contributions, academic quality, and athletic success. *Contemporary Economic Policy, 18*(2), 248–258.

Ries, L., and Ries, A. (1998). *The 22 immutable laws of branding: How to build a product or service into a world-class brand.* New York: HarperCollins.

Rosen, D. E., Curran, J. M., and Greenlee, T. B. (1998). College choice in a brand elimination framework: The high school student's perspective. *Journal of Marketing for Higher Education, 8*(3), 73–92.

Sack, A. L. (2001, Jan. 26). Big-time athletics vs. academic values: It's a rout. *The Chronicle of Higher Education,* p. B7.

Sack, A. L., and Staurowsky, E. J. (1998). *College athletes for hire: The evolution and legacy of the NCAA's amateur myth.* New York: Praeger.

Sack, A. L., and Watkins, C. (1985). Winning and giving. In D. Chu, J. Segrave, & B. Becker (Eds.), *Sports and higher education* (pp. 299–306). Champaign, IL: Human Kinetics.

Sands, G. C., and Smith, R. J. (1999). Organizing for effective marketing communications in higher education: Restructuring for your competitive edge in marketing. *Journal of Marketing for Higher Education, 9*(2), 41–58.

Savage, H., et al. (1929). *American college athletics.* New York: Carnegie Foundation for the Advancement of Teaching, Bulletin No. 23.

Schevitz, T. (2007, February 2). S. F. State recruits students where they live—MySpace. *San Francisco Chronicle,* B3.

Selingo, J. (2001, Nov. 30). Big game is in president's box. *Chronicle of Higher Education,* A48.

Sevier, R. (2001). Brand as relevance. *Journal of Marketing for Higher Education, 10*(3), 77–96.

Sharp, B., and Dawes, J. (2001). What is differentiation and how does it work? *Journal of Marketing Management, 17*(7–8), 739–759.

Shimp, T. A., Stuart, E. W., and Engle, R. W. (1991). A program of classical conditioning experiments testing variations in the conditioned stimulus and context. *Journal of Consumer Research, 18,* 1–12.

Shulman, J. L., & Bowen, W. G. (2001). *The game of life: College sports and educational values.* Princeton, NJ: Princeton University Press.

Sigelman, L., and Carter, R. (1979). Win one for the giver? Alumni giving and big-time college sports. *Social Science Quarterly, 60,* 284–294.

Silvia, P. J. (2006). *Exploring the psychology of interest.* New York: Oxford University Press.

Slaughter, S., and Leslie, L. L. (1997). *Academic capitalism: Politics, policies, and the entrepreneurial university.* Baltimore: Johns Hopkins University Press.

Smith, R. E., and Swinyard, W. R. (1983). Information response models: An integrated approach. *Journal of Marketing, 46*(1), 81–93.

Spaeth, J. L., and Greeley, A. (1970). *Recent alumni and higher education.* New York: McGraw-Hill.

Sperber, M. (1990). *College sports, inc.: The athletic department vs. the university.* New York: Henry Holt.

Sperber, M. (1998). *Onward to victory: The crisis that shaped college sports.* New York: Henry Holt.

Sperber, M. (2000). *Beer and circus: How big-time college sports is crippling undergraduate education.* New York: Henry Holt.

Stage, F. K., and Hossler, D. (1989). Differences in family influences on college attendance plans for male and female ninth graders. *Research in Higher Education, 30*(3), 301–315.

Stoner, M. (2004). How the web can speak to prospective students. *Chronicle of Higher Education, 50*(34), B10.

Strout, E. (2006). Breaking through the noise of a crowded field. *Chronicle of Higher Education, 52*(37), A26.

Suggs, W. (2001, Mar. 30). Study casts doubt on idea that winning teams yield more applicants. *The Chronicle of Higher Education,* p. A51.

Tedeschi, B. (2004, Sept. 23). College recruiters lure students with new online tools. *New York Times,* p. E5.

Telander, R. (1996). *The hundred yard lie: The corruption of college football and what we can do to stop it.* Champaign: University of Illinois Press.

Thacker, L. (2005). Confronting the commercialization of admissions. *Chronicle of Higher Education, 51*(25), B26.

Tinto, V. (1987). *Leaving college: Rethinking the causes and cures of student attrition.* Chicago: University of Chicago Press.

Toma, J. D. (2006). Necessary infrastructure—Or mission inflation? *Chronicle of Higher Education, 52*(21), B10.

Toma, J. D., and Cross, M. E. (1998). Intercollegiate athletics and student college choice: Exploring the impact of championship seasons on undergraduate applications. *Research in Higher Education, 39*(6), 633–661.

Toma, J. D., Dubrow, G., and Hartley, M. (2005). *The uses of institutional culture: Strengthening identification and building brand equity in higher education.* ASHE Higher Education Report, *31*(2). San Francisco: Jossey-Bass.

Topor, R. S. (1986). *Institutional image: How to define, improve, market it.* Washington, DC: Council for Advancement and Support of Education.

Underwood, J. (1980, May 19). Student-athletes: The sham and the shame. *Sports Illustrated,* pp. 36–73.

Wasmer, D. J., and Bruner, G. C. (1999). The antecedents of the market orientation in higher education. *Journal of Marketing for Higher Education, 9*(2), 93–105.

Weissman, J. (1990). Institutional image assessment and modification in colleges and universities. *Journal for Higher Education Management, 6,* 65–75.

Winston, G. C. (1999). Subsidies, hierarchy, and peers: The awkward economics of higher education. *Journal of Economic Perspectives, 13*(1), 13–36.

Winter, G. (2003, Oct. 5). Jacuzzi U.? A battle of perks to lure students. *New York Times,* A12.

Wright, P. (1980). Message-evoked thoughts: Persuasion research using thought verbalizations. *Journal of Consumer Research, 7,* 557–580.

Zajonc, R. B. (1968). Attitudinal effects of mere exposure. *Journal of Personality and Social Psychology, 9,* Monograph supplement No. 2, Part 2.

Zemsky, R., and Oedel, P. (1983). *The structure of college choice.* New York: College Board.

Zemsky, R., Wegner, G. R., and Massy, W. F. (2005). *Remaking the American university: Market-smart and mission-centered.* Piscataway, NJ: Rutgers University Press.

Zimbalist, A. (1999). *Unpaid professionals: Commercialism and conflict in big-time college sports.* Princeton, NJ: Princeton University Press.

Name Index

A
Aaker, D. A., 35, 36
Adelman, C., 81, 82
Adenekan, S., 87
Agres, S. J., 14
Andre, J., 68
Antonio, A. L., 93
Armstrong, G., 51, 77, 98
Arnoldy, B., 54, 57

B
Baade, R. A., 74
Backer, H. W., 35
Baker, W. E., 42, 43
Ballinger, P., 65
Barban, A. M., 46
Bartlett, T., 46
Bates, R., 35
Bauerly, R. J., 45, 46, 47
Bay, D., 91, 92
Berla, N., 11
Berry, L., 95, 96
Best, R., 51
Bierley, C., 43
Blackscon, M., 41
Blumenstyk, G., 3, 23, 27
Bok, D., 4, 20, 21, 24, 28, 29, 44, 55
Bontrager, R. M., 67
Bornstein, R. F., 42
Bowen, W. G., 68, 71
Braxton, J., 10, 11, 12
Brock, T. C., 14, 16

Broekemier, G. M., 58, 59
Bruner, C. G., 91, 95

C
Cabrera, A. F., 10, 11, 12
Cacioppo, J. T., 6, 9, 14, 16
Canterbury, R. M., 5, 31, 99
Capraro, A. J., 58, 59, 95
Carlson, S., 58
Carnevale, D., 21, 22, 24, 28, 80, 84
Carter, R., 66, 75
Chapman, D. W., 10, 11
Chu, D., 66
Chute, E., 10
Ciba, D., 96
Clinton, R. J., 94
Cobb-Walgren, C. J., 35, 36
Coccari, R. I., 95
Cohen, A. M., 61, 62
Conard, M. A., 57
Conard, M. J., 57
Conklin, M.E., 11
Cooper, S. W., 94
Coopersmith, G., 10, 11, 12
Cox, J., 80, 81
Curran, J. M., 94

D
Dahlin-Brown, N., 54
Dailey, A. R., 11
Dale, B. G., 80, 81
Daniel, H., 91, 92

Subject Index

A

Access, providing convenient, 52
Advertising. *See* marketing and advertising
Affective conditioning, 42, 43
Alumni, motivating, 73–74
Amenities, as tangible features, 38–39
American InterContintal University, 21
Apollo Group, 23
Apple iPod, 34
Athletics programs: aspects of visible,
   63–64; branding community and, 45;
   buying success through, 74–75; calls for
   reform in, 68; costs of advertising,
   65–67; costs of maintaining, 72; effects
   of success of, 66–67; halo effect of, 38,
   60–76; intercollegiate versus big-time,
   67–76; link between winning and giving
   through, 74–75; professional sports
   versus college, 70; as public
   entertainment, 70–71, 76; role of, 68,
   71–72; status elevation through, 75;
   theories on popularity as advertising
   mechanisms, 73
Attitudinal responses to message, 16
Availability, 51
Awareness, 91

B

Bayh-Dole Act, 21
The Best 266 Colleges, 55
Brands/branding: actions taken on, 41;
   advertising and, 42; avoiding need for

rebranding, 42; brand communities,
44–45, 74; deception in, 40; elements
of, 35–42; functions of, 31; literature
on, 41; message of, 39; products versus,
36; strategy steps for, 40–42, 41–42;
successful, 47, 98
Business marketing strategies, 17–18
Business model of operation, 3–4

C

Campus amenities, 57–60
Campus culture: effect of athletics
   programs on, 72; promoting desired, 2
Campus visits, 93–94
Canon, 33
Central route of message processing, 14
Chapman's model for choosing a college, 10
Choice Stage of college choice process, 11
Choosing a college. *See* college choice
The Chronicle of Higher Education, 23, 56
Cognitive aspects of college choice, 16–17
Cognitive Response Theory, 16–17
Collaborative partners, 91–94
College choice: Chapman's model, 10;
   cognitive aspects of, 16–17; Elaboration
   Likelihood Model, 13–18; emotional
   aspects of, 93; establishing distinction
   for, 100; factors contributing to, 11–12;
   literature on, 10, 11; magnitude of
   decision in, 92–93; stages of process of,
   11; subconscious reasons for, 67
College rankings, 53–57, 78–79; ranking

P

Parents: functions in college choice of, 11–12; rating of institutional characteristics, 34
Peripheral route of message processing, 14–15
Personal involvement, in information processing, 15
Persuasion model. *See* Elaboration Likelihood Model
Phoenix, University of, 21, 22–23
Photographs in marketing materials, 77
Podcasts, 85
Positioning strategies, 24; as social institutions, 2
Positive image, 33–35
Postsecondary education, 6–7
Predispositional Stage of college choice process, 11
Prestige, 13, 83
Price, providing a better, 52
Product: brand versus, 36; as opportunity concept, 5, 99; providing a better, 51
Professional sports versus college athletics programs, 70
Profitability of commercial higher education, 23
Promotional materials and communication: digital engagement, 84–88; focus/content of, 93; niche marketing, 76–77, 78–79; photographs, 77; viewbooks, 78–84; Web sites and Internet as, 80–84

Q

Quality, perceptions of, 66

R

Rebranding: avoiding need for, 43; reasons for, 43–44
Recommendations for selling. *See* marketing strategies
Recreation centers, 57–58
Relationship marketing, 95–97

Reputation: role of, 35. *See also* college rankings

S

Search Stage of college choice process, 11
Second Life, 85
Service, providing better, 51
Slogans, 45–47; rules for writing, 46–47
Social institutions, positioning colleges and universities as, 2
Social life, 57–60, 79
Social networking sites online, 84–85
Sports. *See* athletics programs
Stakeholders: building trust/engaging, 12–13; internal, 40
State schools, funding for, 2
Students: as collaborative partners, 92; as customers/product, 3, 13, 91–92; digital engagement of, 84–88; as learners versus customers, 26; nontraditional, 22; as online ambassadors, 86

T

Tangibility of education as product, 98; categories of, 32
Television exposure, 67–76, 69
Texas, University of, 17, 60
Traditional higher education, compared to online, 28, 29
Trust economy, 18

U

University of Maryland, 43–44
University of Nebraska, 17
University of Phoenix, 21, 22–23
University of Texas, 17, 60
U.S. News & World Report: college rankings, 54, 56–57; ranking reports, 42

V

Value, providing better, 52
Viability of institutions, 98
Viewbooks, 78–84
Virtual presence online, 80–84

W

Washington State University, 17
The Washington Monthly College
    Rankings, 55
Web logs (blogs), 84–85
Web sites: assumptions about design and
    content, 83–84; college rankings, 55; as
    marketing resources, 80–84;
    promotional materials and
    communication via, 78

Y

Yale University, 42
YouTube, 86

About the Author

Eric J. Anctil is assistant professor of education at the University of Portland. He received his Ph.D. in educational leadership and policy analysis from the University of Wisconsin–Madison and holds a bachelor's degree from the University of Oregon and a master's degree from Portland State University. Anctil conducts research on the relationship between K–20 education and media (television, radio, print, the Internet, technology, and other media forms), with a particular emphasis on athletics.

About the ASHE Higher Education Report Series

Since 1983, the ASHE (formerly ASHE-ERIC) Higher Education Report Series has been providing researchers, scholars, and practitioners with timely and substantive information on the critical issues facing higher education. Each monograph presents a definitive analysis of a higher education problem or issue, based on a thorough synthesis of significant literature and institutional experiences. Topics range from planning to diversity and multiculturalism, to performance indicators, to curricular innovations. The mission of the Series is to link the best of higher education research and practice to inform decision making and policy. The reports connect conventional wisdom with research and are designed to help busy individuals keep up with the higher education literature. Authors are scholars and practitioners in the academic community. Each report includes an executive summary, review of the pertinent literature, descriptions of effective educational practices, and a summary of key issues to keep in mind to improve educational policies and practice.

The Series is one of the most peer reviewed in higher education. A National Advisory Board made up of ASHE members reviews proposals. A National Review Board of ASHE scholars and practitioners reviews completed manuscripts. Six monographs are published each year and they are approximately 120 pages in length. The reports are widely disseminated through Jossey-Bass and John Wiley & Sons, and they are available online to subscribing institutions through Wiley InterScience (http://www.interscience.wiley.com).

Call for Proposals

The ASHE Higher Education Report Series is actively looking for proposals. We encourage you to contact one of the editors, Dr. Kelly Ward (kaward@wsu.edu) or Dr. Lisa Wolf-Wendel (lwolf@ku.edu), with your ideas.

Recent Titles

ASHE Higher Education Report
Order Form
SUBSCRIPTIONS AND SINGLE ISSUES

DISCOUNTED BACK ISSUES:

Use this form to receive **20% off** all back issues of ASHE Higher Education Report. All single issues priced at **$22.40** (normally $29.00)

TITLE	ISSUE NO.	ISBN
_____	_____	_____
_____	_____	_____
_____	_____	_____

Call 888-378-2537 or see mailing instructions below. When calling, mention the promotional code, JB7ND, to receive your discount.

SUBSCRIPTIONS: *(1 year, 6 issues)*

☐ New Order   ☐ Renewal

U.S.	☐ Individual: $165	☐ Institutional: $209
Canada/Mexico	☐ Individual: $165	☐ Institutional: $269
All Others	☐ Individual: $201	☐ Institutional: $320

Call 888-378-2537 or see mailing and pricing instructions below. Online subscriptions are available at *www.interscience.wiley.com.*

Copy or detach page and send to:
**John Wiley & Sons, Journals Dept., 5th Floor
989 Market Street, San Francisco, CA 94103-1741**

Order Form can also be faxed to: 888-481-2665

Issue/Subscription Amount: $ _____
Shipping Amount: $ _____
(for single issues only—subscription prices include shipping)
Total Amount: $ _____

SHIPPING CHARGES:

SURFACE	Domestic	Canadian
First Item	$5.00	$6.00
Each Add'l Item	$3.00	$1.50

(No sales tax for U.S. subscriptions. Canadian residents, add GST for subscription orders. Individual rate subscriptions must be paid by personal check or credit card. Individual rate subscriptions may not be resold as library copies.)

☐ Payment enclosed (U.S. check or money order only. All payments must be in U.S. dollars.)

☐ VISA ☐ MC ☐ Amex # _____ Exp. Date _____

Card Holder Name _____ Card Issue # _____

Signature _____ Day Phone _____

☐ Bill Me (U.S. institutional orders only. Purchase order required.)

Purchase order # _____
Federal Tax ID13559302   GST 89102 8052

Name _____

Address _____

Phone _____ E-mail _____

JB7ND

ASHE-ERIC HIGHER EDUCATION REPORT IS NOW AVAILABLE ONLINE AT WILEY INTERSCIENCE

What is Wiley InterScience?

Wiley InterScience is the dynamic online content service from John Wiley & Sons delivering the full text of over 300 leading scientific, technical, medical, and professional journals, plus major reference works, the acclaimed Current Protocols laboratory manuals, and even the full text of select Wiley print books online.

What are some special features of Wiley InterScience?

Wiley Interscience Alerts is a service that delivers table of contents via e-mail for any journal available on Wiley InterScience as soon as a new issue is published online.
Early View is Wiley's exclusive service presenting individual articles online as soon as they are ready, even before the release of the compiled print issue. These articles are complete, peer-reviewed, and citable.
CrossRef is the innovative multi-publisher reference linking system enabling readers to move seamlessly from a reference in a journal article to the cited publication, typically located on a different server and published by a different publisher.

How can I access Wiley InterScience?

Visit http://www.interscience.wiley.com.

Guest Users can browse Wiley InterScience for unrestricted access to journal Tables of Contents and Article Abstracts, or use the powerful search engine.
Registered Users are provided with a *Personal Home Page* to store and manage customized alerts, searches, and links to favorite journals and articles. Additionally, Registered Users can view free Online Sample Issues and preview selected material from major reference works.
Licensed Customers are entitled to access full-text journal articles in PDF, with select journals also offering full-text HTML.

How do I become an Authorized User?

Authorized Users are individuals authorized by a paying Customer to have access to the journals in Wiley InterScience. For example, a University that subscribes to Wiley journals is considered to be the Customer.

Faculty, staff and students authorized by the University to have access to those journals in Wiley InterScience are Authorized Users. Users should contact their Library for information on which Wiley journals they have access to in Wiley InterScience.

ASK YOUR INSTITUTION ABOUT WILEY INTERSCIENCE TODAY!

Complete online access for your institution

Register for complimentary online access to *Journal of Leadership Studies* today!